D1616368

Sarris costume illustration by Gina DeDomenico

05 791.4372
MCA

Published by Hero Collector Books,
a division of Eaglemoss Ltd. 2021
Premier Place, 2 & A Half
Devonshire Square, EC2M 4UJ,
London, UK.

Eaglemoss France, 144 Avenue
Charles de Gaulle, 92200
Neuilly-Sur-Seine

TM Paramount Pictures.
© 2021 DW Studios, LLC.
All rights reserved.

All rights reserved. No part of
this publication may be reproduced,
stored in a retrieval system or
transmitted in any form or by any
means, electronic, mechanical,
photocopying, recording or
otherwise, without the prior
permission of the publisher.

ILM photos and concept design
© Industrial Light & Magic.
Used with Permission.

All Stan Winston Studio concept
design & behind-the-scenes images
appearing in this book are copyright
© 1999 Stan Winston Studio.
All rights reserved.

w w w . h e r o c o l l e c t o r . c o m

ISBN 978-1-85875-972-2
10 9 8 7 6 5 4 3 2 1

Printed in China

AUGUST 2021

THE INSIDE STORY

MATT McALLISTER
FOREWORD BY DEAN PARISOT

eaglemoss
HERO COLLECTOR

CARLSBAD
CITY LIBRARY
Carlsbad, CA
92011
DISCARD

FOREWORD
BY DEAN PARISOT

When you make a movie you obviously hope that people will enjoy it, but you never know if it's going to stand the test of time. Are viewers likely to still be watching it a year or two down the line? Will they remember it in 10 or even 20 years? I'm as astounded as anyone to say that with *Galaxy Quest*, the answer seems to be a resounding yes. To have people say, "Oh, I love that movie!" after more than two decades is hugely rewarding and a testament to the entire group who helped craft it.

For a start, there was David Howard's great story and Bob Gordon's brilliant script. It was such a wonderfully absurd and offbeat sci-fi adventure tale. I loved the high-stakes emotional payoffs for all of its characters and the heartfelt tribute to fans, and, of course, it was incredibly funny. I was a fan of *Star Trek* growing up, and I loved how Bob was able to both mock and celebrate the conventions of that TV show and of the fans who adored it. But what really impressed me was that Bob's script was about something more universal. It celebrated the filmmaking process and our ability to suspend disbelief. That quality we all have to emotionally lose ourselves in a movie or TV show, to ignore the contrivance and connect to the characters and their story. In that respect, I guess we're all like the Thermians.

And then there was the cast. Tim Allen was hysterical, and so adept at discovering the emotional truth of that character's damaged ego. And I was so incredibly lucky to have assembled the rest of those amazing performers: Sigourney Weaver, the dearly missed Alan Rickman, Tony Shalhoub, Sam Rockwell, Daryl Mitchell, Enrico Colantoni, Justin Long… the list goes on. It was an absolute delight to work with this level of talent.

If not for the producer of *Galaxy Quest*, my friend Mark Johnson, none of it would have happened. From his initial belief in Bob Gordon to write the script, to orchestrating the movie, Mark always supported the filmmakers and fought for what we needed. The production and postproduction team were, and still are, stellar. The film benefited hugely from David Newman's perfect score, Jerzy Zieliński's beautiful cinematography, and Don Zimmerman's flawless editing, to mention just a few names. Many of the people who worked on *Galaxy Quest* have worked with me again in the years since, and I am grateful to all of them.

I should mention the visual effects as well, which at that time were old-school practical effects meets CGI. I had never done a big effects movie before *Galaxy Quest*, so it was a learning curve. But I had spent my childhood reading and watching science fiction and was fascinated by how it all worked. I had experimented with anything I could assemble or disassemble so it was tremendous fun to watch the Stan Winston Studio and ILM create those magical creatures and ships.

In this book, you'll hear from many of the very talented people who helped make *Galaxy Quest* such a unique movie, and see some of the concept art behind the film's marvelous monsters, sets, and spaceships. I think I can say we all thoroughly enjoyed the process of making *Galaxy Quest*. Creating any movie is a team effort and our cast and crew did an incredible job making this film – a film I'm hopeful fans will still be watching in another two decades' time.

Dean Parisot

Dean Parisot (center) on the
Galaxy Quest set with producer
Mark Johnson (left) and executive
producer Steven Spielberg (right).

CAPTAIN STARSHINE

David Howard was an office temp who dreamed of making it big in Hollywood. His chances of success were roughly 1 in 10,000. Then he had a wild idea…

"CAPTAIN STARSHINE"

An Original Screenplay

By

David Howard

The hero of *Captain Starshine* was transported to the other side of the Galaxy by aliens.

Registered WGA

A N IMAGE OF JUPITER FLICKERED onto the cinema screen. A few seconds later, came a voice, solemn yet reassuringly familiar. "Will we leave our home on Earth for other worlds?" asked the voice. "The distances are vast. The voyage hazardous…"

Sitting in the audience at the IMAX in Los Angeles was office temp and struggling writer David Howard. It was 1994, and Howard was in attendance to see a short film about the African Serengeti as research for a play he was working on. But it was the trailer for *Americans in Space*, a documentary about the US Space Program, that caught his attention. "I said to myself, 'I know that voice...' and tried to place it," Howard recalls. "Then I realized, 'Oh, it's Leonard Nimoy.' It made me think about how hopelessly typecast actors like that can be. Even when they don't appear on camera! It struck me as kind of funny and tragic in a way. I just started exploring what it must be like to be trapped in that sort of situation."

After mulling the idea over for a few days, Howard sat down to begin a script for a movie. The script was *Captain Starshine*. Five years later, it had undergone a metamorphosis to become *Galaxy Quest*.

STRANGE NEW WORLDS

Like many Americans, Howard had grown up watching *Star Trek* in syndication as a kid in Tucson, Arizona. "It was on dinnertime every night, and my sister and I would watch it over and over again," he remembers. "I loved the show, though I like to describe myself as a Trekkie-once-removed because there are others – like my sister – who were into it more than I was."

When Howard was 16, Gene Roddenberry came to speak at a local science fiction convention. "I remember Roddenberry telling us how much the situation had changed since *Star Trek* had been cancelled. He had gone back to Paramount a number of times to try and get something new happening for several years, and was always shut down. But by the time he spoke to us, the shoe was on

In Howard's script, the cult TV star-turned-hero was named Richard Skylar, while the lead alien was Cardox from the planet Aldensia.

As in *Galaxy Quest*, the aliens of *Captain Starshine* believed the show to be "historical documents" and its characters to be very real.

the other foot. Paramount was coming to *him* to develop new *Star Trek* programming. What was most exciting was the feeling that *Star Trek* was far from dead, and there were many more strange new worlds yet to explore. Thinking back, that was the beginning right there of this devotion to the world."

Howard's memories of *Star Trek* – and the show's cast – fed into his *Captain Starshine* script. "It was about a guy hopelessly mired in the role of being this sci-fi hero," he says. "The main character wanted to be a serious actor, and the script began with him doing a reading for Mark Antony in *Julius Caesar*. It cut to the director and stage manager watching him. The stage manager goes, 'He's really good.' And the director says, 'He is. Are we going to cast him?' The stage manager replies, 'Are you kidding? He's Captain Starshine.'"

Howard's initial notion centered on a TV star, Richard Skylar, who gradually begins to embrace a role he has long viewed as a millstone around his neck. There was plenty of potential for a quirky character piece. Yet it became something far more high-concept when Howard hit upon the idea of aliens showing up at a convention that Captain Starshine is attending and beaming him into space –

without him even realizing what's happening. "From there, it kind of wrote itself," Howard says.

Over the next eight months, Howard hammered out the first draft of his script, furiously writing while waiting for the phone to ring in his various temp positions. While the concept of *Captain Starshine* would carry over into *Galaxy Quest*, there were some fundamental differences in Howard's draft – not least in its antagonist. "The 'second banana' guy in my script – the equivalent to Spock or the Alexander Dane character – has his own little sci-fi franchise, a little like Walter Koenig does. He's written all these novels and made a lot of money out of it, which he has poured into trying to find a way to connect with other dimensions. He opens up a rift and goes through to this other planet. But he's like this snake in the Garden of Eden. Everyone is wide-eyed and innocent on this planet, and he becomes a Ming the Merciless-type usurper who takes over. Then these spies hear about how he hates this Captain Starshine character, which is why they go and find him. My script felt a little more *Flash Gordon*. But as a friend of mine said, 'Your story is really different. But it's also really the same.'"

THE STARS ALIGN

Howard eventually finished a draft he was happy with. There was just one problem: he had never sold a script before. "I was a nobody," he says. But then he showed it to his friend Sona Gourgouris, who had recently left her job as production executive at the production company Beacon Pictures. "Sona read my script and said, 'You know, I think someone would make this. I think we could set this up.'"

Gourgouris took the script to Suzann Ellis, a former colleague at Beacon. Ellis – who, like Gourgouris, would become co-producer on *Galaxy Quest* – then liaised with various talent agencies over the next year. "At the same time, we were polishing the script. I sent it to Sona and Suzann, they'd give me notes, and we'd make it tighter."

Everything changed when Ellis passed on the script to Mark Ross, an agent at the influential talent agency CAA. Ross immediately spotted the script's potential. "*Men in Black* had recently opened and been a huge hit," Howard says. "The agency had a big meeting where someone asked, 'Where's the next sci-fi comedy hit after *Men in Black*?' Mark said, 'I got it right here. It's called *Captain Starshine*...'"

Before long, Ross was championing the script around town.

The concept caught the attention of independent producer Mark Johnson, who had a first-look deal at DreamWorks, the fledgling company formed a few years earlier by Steven Spielberg, Jeffrey Katzenberg, and David Geffen. "DreamWorks had recently had a family film project scheduled for release in Christmas 1999 that fell apart," Howard recalls. "They were looking for something to fast track when our script came through the door."

For Howard, the idea that one of his wild ideas had somehow evolved into a major Hollywood production is as outlandish as the plot of *Galaxy Quest*. "Suzann Ellis said to me afterward, 'David, do you realize this is a 1-in-10,000 chance? It doesn't happen that someone writes a spec and it becomes a major feature.' It's like a pinball game where all the gates have to be open to get to that one place at the top where you win a free game. My script came to DreamWorks at the exact time when they needed to make movies at a time when *Men in Black* had just opened. And of course, it turned out to be such a great film. It was such a brilliant piece of collaboration: the tone that Dean Parisot brought to it, Robert Gordon's final script, everything that the actors added... I'm honored to have my name associated with it." ◆

In Howard's script the Dane-type "second banana" character, Vincent, was the film's villain, while the fictional TV show was called *The Starshine Chronicles*.

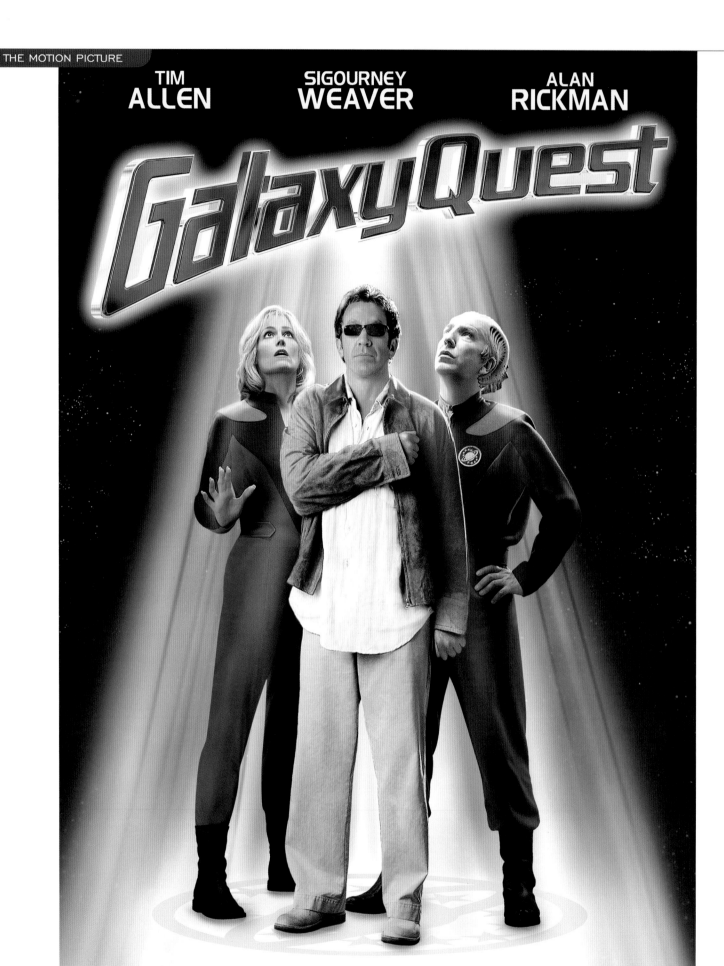

Galaxy Quest poster depicting a hungover-looking Jason Nesmith with Gwen DeMarco and Alexander Dane.

GALAXY QUEST
THE MOTION PICTURE

After DreamWorks optioned *Captain Starshine* in 1997, producer Mark Johnson and executive producer Elizabeth Cantillon sought out writers to develop the story. Enter Robert Gordon, a *Star Trek* fan with a new spin on the material.

"**I** WAS AN UNLIKELY PERSON TO DO IT," admits Mark Johnson, the Oscar®-winning producer behind such hits as *Rain Man* and *Good Morning Vietnam*. "I'm not sure I'd even seen a full episode of *Star Trek*. But what I responded to, of course, was not the science fiction element of it but the whole notion of the insecurity and rivalry of actors."

At the time, DreamWorks was looking to option scripts that would establish the studio as a major player in the movie industry. When Johnson's colleague, Tiffany Daniel, brought him the outline for David Howard's *Captain Starshine*, he knew it fitted the bill. "We loved the idea," Johnson says.

DreamWorks swiftly optioned the script, and Johnson turned to executive producer Elizabeth Cantillon to help him develop the project. "They showed me this spoof of *Star Trek* that they had optioned and said, 'Do you think this is a good idea for a movie?'" Cantillon recalls. "I said, yes! But it was really just the premise. So we went out to a bunch of writers to see who responded to it."

Robert Gordon – the screenwriter behind the 1997 rom-com *Addicted to Love* – immediately caught Cantillon and Johnson's attention. Whereas other writers went down the route of the Captain being a prisoner of the role ("We called it the Bill Murray version," says Cantillon, indicating the ideal actor for this version of the character), Gordon pitched them a different take. "Bob Gordon's idea was the opposite, that he *loves* being the Captain," Cantillon continues. "If he could become the Captain again, it would be the best day of his life. That adjustment was such a fresh idea: someone who didn't feel

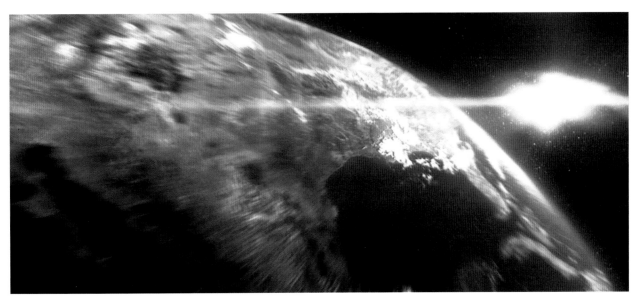

It was writer Robert Gordon's idea to expand the story beyond Earth into outer space.

Writer Robert Gordon (left) with director Dean Parisot and cinematographer Jerzy Zieliński.

imprisoned by the role but empowered by it. It was also Bob's idea to go into outer space... He came up with this whole world."

If Mark Johnson wasn't a huge *Star Trek* fan, then Robert Gordon most certainly was. So when he saw a one-line logline in a writing assignment list ("It said something like, 'Aliens think that William Shatner is Captain Kirk and enlist his help'"), he became excited about what he could do with the material. "Elizabeth said that the main character would be living in the Midwest trying to hide out from his status as this legendary television actor," Gordon recalls. "Then aliens would approach him thinking he was a real space hero and he would try to hide them. It sounded to me like a small-town farce, a bit like *Doc Hollywood*. I think the main reason they brought me in was because the only other movie I had done was a smallish romantic comedy. I don't think they realized I was a huge science fiction fan!"

One of the key movies the producers referenced during Gordon's first meeting now seems rather surprising. "They said the tone should be like the Kevin Kline movie, *In & Out*. I still haven't seen it, but it's a gentle comedy of mistaken identities. I immediately said, 'It's got to go

to space. You need space battles!' There wasn't a crew either [in the original premise]; it revolved around one character. My starting point was: 'What if real people were put into *The Wrath of Khan*?'"

Gordon went away and mulled over the concept. He knew this could be the perfect project for him. But the writing process proved to be neither quick nor straightforward. "It was really difficult," Gordon admits. "Not only is there the crew but you've got their alter egos. I firstly went through every crew position in *Star Trek*... Is there a Worf character? Is there an empath? Is there a bartender? I went through the list, but some of those characters already seemed a bit of a parody to me. Once I had settled on the positions of the characters, I thought, 'What's the most fun or the most dramatic way to complement that kind of character with their personality?'"

Something Gordon was clear about from the start was that this couldn't simply be a *Star Trek* takeoff. After all, as Gordon points out, there had already been dozens of such parodies. "I wanted it to be its own thing that had the heart and soul of *Star Trek* but wasn't literal, pointy-ears *Star Trek*. It had to have verisimilitude. It had to have emotional integrity." In fact, Gordon's research extended to watching ensemble dramas as much as sci-fi, including *The Untouchables* and *The Magnificent Seven*, knowing that he needed to perfect the dynamics among the crew to pull off the emotional integrity.

Yet as the weeks rolled by, Gordon found himself struggling to combine his ideas into a coherent whole. He received phone calls from Cantillon and Tiffany Daniel to see how he was doing. Fine, he told them. He loved the project, he was working hard on it… but he didn't have it yet. Another week passed. Another phone call. "I don't think I realized that they were interviewing other writers!" Gordon laughs. "I was in a bubble, thinking, 'Well, of course, *they're only*

talking to me.' I mean, they were very encouraging. But another week, and I may not have been the writer."

Gordon remembers asking Cantillon if he could read the *Captain Starshine* script, hoping it might spark ideas. "Elizabeth said, 'It would probably be better if you weren't influenced by it.' So I never read it until after the movie was done."

Gradually, though, Gordon's take on the story began to coalesce. The inner life of his characters and the themes of the film seemed clearer now. "It became a story about friendship, with a lead character who represents these ideals that you want to believe in. You believe in Jason because, deep down, Gwen believes he's a good guy."

Jason and Gwen share a kiss in the final act of *Galaxy Quest*, part of a series of character payoffs that Gordon built into the story.

Early concept art depicting Sarris, Gorignak, and the pig lizard by Stan Winston Studio artist Simon Bisley.

Copyright © 1999 Stan Winston Studio

Gordon adds that he tried not to picture William Shatner while writing Jason. "I was thinking of a Charlton Heston kind of character – *The Omega Man* is one of my favorite movies." Gwen, meanwhile, was written as "someone who had real chops as an actress, but was cast in the kind of 'serve coffee and exposition' part women were often relegated to in the earlier days of science fiction." In contrast, Alexander Dane was inspired by the great Alec Guinness – "an actor who famously didn't like how silly his character was in *Star Wars*."

Besides the crew, Gordon realized he needed to introduce fans as key characters for the story to work. "I wanted to celebrate fandom. Everything revolves around people believing in other people, and it's formalized in the way the fans believe in the show and in Jason. They want it to be real and so does the audience."

This theme of belief, of course, extends to *Galaxy Quest*'s naïve, good-natured aliens. The Thermians – their name was intended to

be a nod to 'theremin' – believe in the show even more literally than the fans. It was very important to Gordon that these aliens were not simply one-note walking gags; they needed to have a life of their own. "I started to build an emotional reality for the Thermians, where they weren't just ciphers. I wanted the audience to really believe that they built their entire way of life, their culture, on this TV show – or 'historical documents,' which was one of David Howard's ideas."

After building up his cast of characters, Gordon began weaving satisfying payoffs for each of them into his narrative. "Take Fred – or 'Dusty,' as he was in my early drafts. What's interesting about him isn't that he's oblivious, but rather that he has these defense mechanisms that he's used to protect himself his whole life. He has to figure out how he's going to [pretend] to be the smartest guy in the world – which he does by delegating the problem to the Thermians. But then there comes a point where he can't delegate anymore and has to save Jason by using the molecular conveyor. That's his crisis point. When I got to that point with a character, I could check them off the list, even if I wasn't sure how everything was going to be resolved necessarily. Scenes like that began to click."

Gordon began to devise set pieces, too – and as with the characters, it was crucial for him to ground these in reality. "The scene of Tommy taking the ship out of dock is a classic *Star Trek: The Motion Picture* concept. But I was thinking of someone taking their car out of a parking space... they don't see a pole and just hear this scrape. It was something everybody could relate to."

While story and character elements like this gave Gordon increasing confidence about his take on the material, the point where he felt like everything *really* fell into place was when he formulated his 'all is lost' moment – the part of a narrative where a hero comes closer to achieving his goals after enduring a period of pain and high emotion. "Once I came up with the scene where Sarris forces Jason to tell the Thermians that he's a fraud and not the hero they thought he was, I knew the shape of the movie."

Structure, characters, and story beats completed, Gordon pitched his take on the material to DreamWorks. "There was a big table," he remembers. "They were all really nice. There was fruit. But I'm always extremely nervous about that sort of stuff. I sweated a whole bunch and pitched the story out of order."

Despite this, the studio loved it and Gordon went away to write the first full draft of *Galaxy Quest: The Motion Picture* (as he originally titled it). It took seven weeks... "Then I sat on it for a week to work out if I'd got insane writing it." Very soon afterward, DreamWorks green-lit the project. *Galaxy Quest* was making the hyperjump from page to screen. "I was super excited," says Gordon. "But I was also like, 'What's the catch?' I mean, my first romantic comedy took 10 years [in development]. Then I heard that Harold Ramis wanted to make *Galaxy Quest*. It was the very-best-case scenario…" ✦

Gordon expanded the characters beyond the captain to introduce a full crew who were inspired by some of the positions seen in *Star Trek*.

THE QUEST
BEGINS

GALAXY QUEST

DIRECTED BY HAROLD RAMIS

8/10/98

It seemed to be going so well. A big-name director was in place, sets were being built, and everyone felt they were onto something special – until a disagreement over casting threw the production into disarray.

EVERYONE LOVED HAROLD RAMIS. LITTLE WONDER: THE WRITER-director-actor-comedian had had a hand in some of the greatest comedy movies of all time: *National Lampoon's Animal House, National Lampoon's Vacation, Stripes, Ghostbusters, Groundhog Day...* So when Ramis signed up to *Galaxy Quest*, the studio and producers felt that the movie's potential had been taken to the next level. "I was so delighted," says Elizabeth Cantillon. "I couldn't believe I was going to produce a movie that Harold was directing."

Ramis's comedy credentials – as well as his experience on *Ghostbusters*, another film that effortlessly blended genres – meant that he was a good fit with the material. "I can't remember what other directors we went out to, but Harold was an obvious choice because he's such a wonderful comedic director," says Mark Johnson. "Having been an actor himself, he understood immediately the [theme of the] nature of actors."

Robert Gordon met with Ramis to discuss the project in the director's hometown of Chicago. "He was everything you thought he'd be," Gordon says. "No pretentions, funny, relaxed. I peppered him with all these annoying fanboy questions about *Ghostbusters* and he was so nice about it."

With a director in place, other key department heads were brought onto the picture. One of the most important roles was the production designer, who would need to bring to life the story's spaceship interiors, alien environments, and fan culture. With Ramis's approval, the producers turned to Linda DeScenna, who had worked with Johnson on everything from *Rain Man* to *Toys,* and also boasted science fiction credentials from her work as set decorator on *Star Trek: The Motion Picture* and *Blade Runner.*

Before DeScenna began designing sets, she visited a *Star Trek* convention in Plano, Texas, to get a deeper feeling for the show. She also had detailed conversations about the look

Warren Manser's concept art of the Thermians' devastated homeworld.

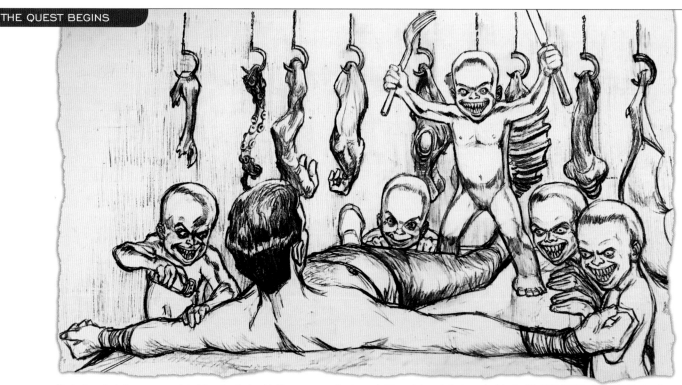

Gordon's early drafts were more violent than the final script. One scene saw the demon babies eat Jason's flesh, as depicted in this 1998 ILM illustration by Benton Jew.

and feel of the film with Ramis. Early on in preproduction, DeScenna and Ramis's take was that the Thermians' technology and culture would have the aesthetic of a 1960s science fiction TV show, rather than the technologically advanced spin on a late-'70s TV show seen in the final film. "We had discussions on how you make a movie look like a TV show without it looking like a bad movie," says DeScenna. "[My work on] *Star Trek: The Motion Picture* was not an influence at all. That had been very modern, very up with the times, very space age. Whereas in my brain, the whole [*Galaxy Quest*] project had the feel of science fiction from the late 1960s. It was supposed to look as if all the sets didn't quite have enough money. I was excited about that as I thought it could look spectacular on screen. I remember my conversations with Harold. It was, 'Oh, this will be so much fun. Remember how the planets looked like they had papier-mâché rocks?' We were kind of laughing about that in the meeting. After the *Star Trek* convention, I came back and started in that direction with my crew, building sets."

Another department head hired early on was Albert Wolsky, the veteran costume designer who had won Oscars® for his work on 1979's *All That Jazz* and 1991's *Bugsy*. It was the job of Wolsky and his crew to design the outfits for the main heroes, as well as for the humanoid Thermians, Sarris's crew, and the fans.

To create the ambitious visual effects, DreamWorks brought in two top companies that had a track record of working with executive producer Steven Spielberg. ILM was hired to realize the *Protector* and the film's other spaceships, as well as the rock monster

Gorignak. It would do this through a combination of old-style model work and modern CGI, under the watch of visual effects supervisor and *Star Trek* veteran, Bill George.

Meanwhile, Stan Winston Studio was hired to design and construct the Thermians, Sarris's prosthetic makeup, and the pig lizard under the supervision of Winston, Shane Mahan, and Christopher Swift. The two effects companies would collaborate to create the demon babies. Other effects work was outsourced to the smaller companies Light Matters and Pacific Title Digital, with visual effects producer Robert Stadd tasked with wrangling the various VFX houses.

WE NEED TO TALK ABOUT KEVIN

The first role that needed to be cast was Jason Nesmith. A host of big-name actors were sent the *Galaxy Quest* script to consider. A host of big-name actors turned it down. "People that Harold knew, people like Steve Martin," says Mark Johnson. "Everybody loved the script, but for some reason we couldn't find someone to play the captain."

Other actors considered for the role included Tim Robbins, Alec Baldwin, Mel Gibson, and Bruce Willis. But Harold Ramis had one person in particular in mind: Kevin Kline – coincidentally enough, the star of *In & Out*, the movie referenced during Robert Gordon's first meeting. "A lot of the notes I got [from Ramis] were about tailoring it for Kevin Kline," recalls Gordon. "I needed to think of him more as a theatrical sort of character – which was a little difficult as it bumped up against my Alexander Dane character. For any other director I might have pushed back a little and tried to argue the point but, you know, I just thought Harold was a genius. Whatever he had in his head, I was fine trying to get there. And he always gave me the impression of, 'If it doesn't work, we'll change it back.' I totally believed in him."

There were a couple of problems with securing Kevin Kline for the lead, though. The first was that DreamWorks co-founder Jeffrey Katzenberg wanted somebody else entirely. "Jeffrey thought Tim Allen was correct for the role," says *Galaxy Quest*'s line producer, Charles Newirth. "Tim had been so great in *The Santa Clause* and other films he had done. But Harold very badly wanted Kevin Kline. Jeffrey to his credit said, 'OK, if you can get Kevin to do it, great. Otherwise, I'd like Tim to do it.' So he was supportive."

The other rather major stumbling block was that Kevin Kline wasn't interested. "We spent quite a few months courting Kevin Kline, who was living in New York, waiting to see if he was going to give us an answer," Newirth continues. "At the same time, we were doing a rewrite on the script, designing the spaceships, designing the sets, all sorts of things. We knew we had a certain time frame to start filming, given the release date that they wanted. In any case, push came to shove and the day came when Kevin Kline called and said, 'You know what, I'm going to pass on this.' So of course,

Jeffrey Katzenberg said, 'OK, let's go get Tim Allen.'"

Kevin Kline may not have been interested, but Tim Allen most definitely was. Not only did he love the humor and heart of the script, but he was a science fiction aficionado. Working with the legendary Harold Ramis was another plus. A lunch was arranged for Allen, Ramis, and Katzenberg to discuss the movie. It did not go well.

Allen remembers the meeting vividly. "We met with him [Ramis], and right in the middle of a piece of toast and some sausage, he said, 'I gotta be honest with you, Tim. I'm not going this direction' – pointing to me. 'I want an action star who can be funny, not a comedian who might be able to do action.' And with that, the fork dropped. The studio head [Katzenberg] that was with me said, 'Can we speak alone?' I stepped away and when I came back, the director was no longer standing there."

Ramis simply could not visualize Allen in the lead and felt he had no choice but to bow out. The decision sent shock waves through the production. A picture with all the hallmarks of being a critical and commercial smash had turned into a picture with all the hallmarks of being "troubled." Sets had been built. Designs were underway. Filming was due to begin in five weeks. Luckily, Mark Johnson knew just the person to step into Ramis's shoes – if only he could be persuaded. ✦

After Kevin Kline turned down the role, Tim Allen was cast as Jason Nesmith. It became one of the actor's most popular screen roles.

NEW DIRECTIONS

Dean Parisot brought wit and warmth to *Galaxy Quest* – but taking
on a half-developed project weeks before filming was no easy task.

BY 1999, DIRECTOR DEAN PARISOT was known for an Oscar®-winning short, an eclectic selection of TV shows that ranged from sitcoms and police procedurals to preschool series, and *Home Fries*, a 1998 romantic comedy starring Drew Barrymore. What he didn't possess was experience helming a $45 million science fiction movie. Nevertheless, Mark Johnson – his producer on *Home Fries* – felt that Parisot's wit and flair for character-driven stories made him perfect for *Galaxy Quest*.

Johnson had, in fact, given Parisot the script to read over early in preproduction to hear his thoughts. "Dean said to me, 'Why don't you ever give me scripts like this? I'd do it in a second,'" Johnson says. But when Johnson did later suggest that Parisot go for the role, he remembers that the filmmaker wasn't so sure. "Dean's a good friend of mine, but sometimes he needs to be kicked into doing things!"

Line produer Charles Newirth recalls running into Parisot's agent Dan Aloni while he and Johnson were shopping at Barney's department store. "Mark said to Dan, 'Dean *needs* to do this movie!' And Dan said, 'I'll get him to do it!' Dean has such a unique and inventive voice… but he can be a little indecisive, thinking about putting things together."

Parisot remembers his early doubts all too well. Taking the reins of a major effects-heavy production with minimal time in preproduction was a challenge, to say the least. "I said no because I thought I'd get killed!" he says. "Bob had written a phenomenal script, an incredibly well-constructed screenplay… But it was too big a movie. It was a big undertaking. And then Mark just worked me over, saying, 'I can get you on this movie right now. We need to find somebody and you're available. I can convince them to put you on it.'"

In the end, Parisot knew he had to accept the role. Now the new director had the small task of getting to grips with a production that had already begun, while familiarizing himself with the complex effects and lining up the rest of the cast. "On a movie that size, with all those visual effects, you'd usually start thinking about it around three months beforehand," says Parisot. "We only had [five] weeks before we were supposed to shoot."

"Dean came in with not a lot of time and it was quite a challenge for him to take on," adds Newirth. "He jumped on a fast-moving train – a train that was pulling out of the station and going down the track at 100 miles per hour. He had to accept certain things that were there already in terms of department heads and whatnot. We had to look through this thick binder of storyboards that had been done for certain sequences. To Dean's credit, he hopped on. He's very wry and funny and sarcastic and has such a big heart, and that made it all doable, you know?"

FINAL PREPARATIONS

During the manic final weeks of preproduction, Parisot worked with the producers to hire the remaining department heads. The Oscar®-nominated Don Zimmerman (*Coming Home*, *Rocky III* and *IV*, *Liar Liar*) was recruited as editor; David Newman (who had also been nominated for an Oscar® for his work on 1997's *Anastasia*) came on as composer; and Jerzy Zieliński, who Parisot had worked with on *Home Fries*, became the director of photography.

Something that made the punishing preproduction window a little less daunting was the fact that Parisot wanted minimal changes to Robert Gordon's script. In fact, changes that Ramis had previously requested were largely abandoned as the script returned to its earlier form. However, Gordon admits that he initially wasn't sure why the director of a small-scale rom-com had been chosen to helm a large-scale sci-fi comedy. "I had been pushing for Stephen Sommers, who had just done this funny underwater movie with a giant octopus [*Deep Rising*]," Gordon remembers. Thankfully, his first meeting with Parisot immediately put him at ease. "I met Dean

Director Dean Parisot on location in Goblin Valley.

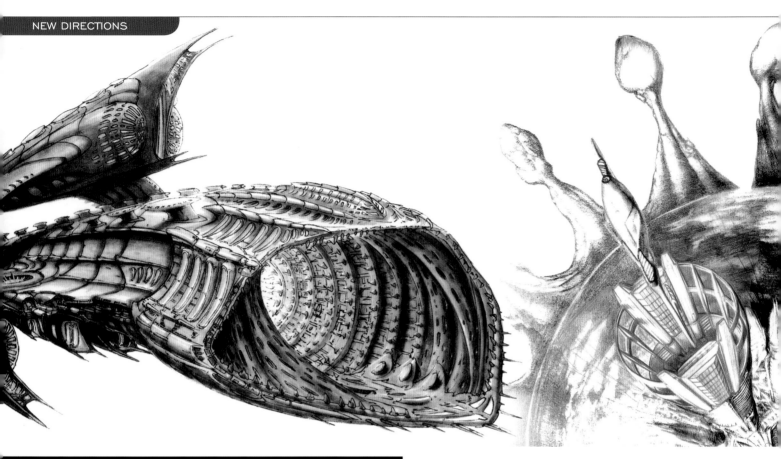

Maquette photo: Profiles in History, www.profilesinhistory.com / Brom concept: Copyright © 1999 Stan Winston Studio

Clockwise from top left: Sarris's ship by Wil Rees; Thermia concept by Warren Manser; Thermian illustration by Stan Winston Studio artist Brom; early rejected Sarris maquette.

When Parisot took over, the set design moved from a 1960s-style aesthetic to one influenced by sci-fi shows from the late 1970s and early 1980s.

and I could not be more thrilled. He just seemed to *get* the tone. I mean a lot of people seemed to have trouble with it – I kept hearing, 'Is it like *Spaceballs*?' Which it's not. But Dean said, 'The script's great, we've got to cut 10 pages out of the ending but that's it.' He had no ego about including me in meetings; he would say, 'I'm glad to have the writer here and we're working in the same direction.' I got super lucky with directors twice, but I can't imagine anyone else directing the film."

Parisot, like Gordon, may have been best known for a modestly budgeted rom-com, but he knew his science fiction. He cites Isaac Asimov's *The Martian Chronicles* and Robert A. Heinlein's *Stranger in a Strange Land* as having a particular impact on him while growing up in Connecticut. Plus, he adored *Star Trek*. "My brothers and I insisted my mother buy this gray station wagon so we could turn it into a spaceship," he laughs. "We decorated it with switches for photon torpedoes and put NCC-1701 on the door." One of Parisot's first jobs out of college even involved directing Geordi La Forge himself, LeVar Burton, in the kids' show, *Reading Rainbow*. "I loved that job!"

GOODBYE TO THE '60S

The basic design of the *Protector* had been approved during Ramis's tenure, and Parisot loved it. However, he did task both the

production illustrators and ILM's art department with creating new, more otherworldly designs for Sarris's ship.

One of the biggest changes that Parisot brought to the film was in the production design, according to Linda DeScenna. The previous 1960s TV show aesthetic of the spacecraft was replaced with one that reflected the Thermians' technologically advanced culture, while the touchstones became sci-fi shows from the late 1970s and early 1980s rather than the 1960s. "All movie sets are crazy, but I've never been on a movie where we changed directors after we'd started building," says DeScenna. "Once Dean came on, there was a rush to change some of the concepts. I think Steven [Spielberg] had been rethinking it, too. I remember he wanted a really shiny floor… It went in a much more *Buck Rogers* and *Battlestar Galactica* direction. We had to make changes as quickly and inexpensively as we could. The corridors had to look slicker. We redesigned the bridge, redesigned the floors. Although, once they did change to the late '70s/'80s theme it was easier in some ways, because [that aesthetic] could be done a little quicker."

PERFECT FIT

The other key element of the film that required Parisot's attention was casting. Of course, one actor was already attached to the project by this point, and Parisot sat down with Tim Allen to see if

Line producer Charles Newirth and Parisot on set; Tim Allen, who Parisot thought was perfect for the role.

they saw eye-to-eye on the character. "I basically said to Tim, 'I'm going to treat this as a drama,'" he remembers. "Tim was like, 'But it's a comedy!'"

Nevertheless, Parisot quickly saw how the comedian was ideal for the role. It was a given that Allen could handle the funny stuff. But Parisot also realized how the character was the perfect fit for an actor famous for a beloved TV show (in Allen's case, *Home Improvement*) that in many ways continued to define him. "Tim could find all of the colors [of the character]. It made sense to me. [During early rehearsals] I watched him fighting, trying to make it more grounded and real. It didn't take him long to embrace it completely. He was fun and hysterical, but he also worked like crazy. There were other names that had been thrown around before Tim was brought on that I guess I could have revisited, but after sitting down with him I said, 'This is the guy!'"

Now Parisot just needed to assemble the rest of his command crew, along with supporting characters, such as the Thermians and the fans. Luckily, he had Debra Zane – his "favorite casting director of all time" – to help him. "I was looking for dramatic actors rather than comic actors," says Parisot – and he found what he was

looking for in the shape of Sigourney Weaver and Alan Rickman as the movie's other leads.

Other actors brought into the ensemble included *Big Night*'s Tony Shalhoub as Fred; Daryl Mitchell – who Parisot pushed for after working with him on *Home Fries* – as Tommy; Enrico Colantoni, Missi Pyle, Patrick Breen, and Jed Rees as the core Thermians; *Buffy the Vampire Slayer*'s Robin Sachs as Sarris; and the then little-known Sam Rockwell as Guy, who Zane vigorously pursued for the role. Some cast members were *complete* unknowns, including Justin Long – a recommendation from Zane's sister Bonnie, who had cast Long in a TV pilot that was never picked up.

"It's difficult to overstate Deb's contribution to the movie," says Robert Gordon. "While writing I had an assortment of faces in my head for each of the characters, but now, years later, I find it impossible to imagine *Galaxy Quest* without this perfect ensemble."

Thanks to Zane, even the tiny parts were filled with brilliant character actors: *Kids in the Hall*'s Kevin McDonald was cast as the announcer during the final sequence (largely improvising his dialogue), while Heidi Swedberg – who unforgettably portrayed George's fiancée Susan in *Seinfeld* – played Brandon's mom.

Less familiar, though no less perfect, was the uncredited performer behind Brandon's dad: *Galaxy Quest*'s video engineer, Ian Kelly.

Parisot is grateful that, despite the short preproduction period, time was built into the schedule for rehearsal with his stellar cast. "Most movies throw you right into the pool now, but rehearsal is so important. During that period, we discovered so many things, like Alan being stuck with this headpiece that was slowly destroyed over the course [of the film]. And we managed to expand Tony's role in rehearsals."

During this period, Parisot naturally used *Star Trek* as one key reference point with his cast, as well as documentaries about fan culture. But he knew it was *Galaxy Quest*'s characters that made Gordon's script really come alive, and the director talked about Earthbound films that centered on "emotionally needy actors," such as *Withnail and I,* as much as science fiction.

With the film cast, new sets built, and visual effects concepts coming together, the potential disaster of losing a director late into preproduction had been averted. Once again, there was a general sense that *Galaxy Quest* could be something special. They were ready to start filming. ✦

Above: The command crew on the bridge – note large "patch" over battle damage in background. Above right: Parisot, Weaver, and Rickman in Goblin Valley.

LIFT OFF!

Over four months in the studio, the *Galaxy Quest* shoot took in everything from frantic rewrites to melting walls. Throughout it all, the camaraderie between the cast and crew never wavered.

PRINCIPAL PHOTOGRAPHY ON *GALAXY Quest* began on April 19, 1999. Three stages at Warner Hollywood Studio were given over to Linda DeScenna's ambitious sets. These largely consisted of spectacular starship interiors, though they also took in Brandon and Kyle's bedrooms and the papier-mâché-heavy sets of the *Galaxy Quest* TV show. Additional sequences, such as the crew's exchange inside the shuttle during the trip to the desert planet, were filmed at Culver Studios in Culver City.

The majority of scenes were filmed on the two stages dedicated to the *Protector* sets, the most spectacular of which was the bridge.

Constructed on a large rotating gimbal, the bridge was designed to jerk the performers around for real whenever the ship was being blasted by mines or missiles. Though neoprene foam was built into the set to counter the risk of performers knocking themselves out, the effect appeared astonishingly violent. "It shook like an earthquake simulator in the museum," recalls associate visual effects supervisor Ben Snow, who oversaw the movie's CGI. "On the *Star Trek* movies they just faked it! And I haven't been on a film where they've used something like that since. But Dean was trying to add grittiness and realism, even though some of the things going on are ridiculous."

Dean Parisot and his lead cast members prepare to film the mess hall sequence.

Stan Winston checks Robin Sachs's costume and makeup; Sarris tortures the original Thermian commander in a sequence on board his dank, green ship.

While the gimbal was an ingenious solution to visualizing life onboard an alien spacecraft, not every design solution was so successful. John Rutchland, the set foreman who oversaw construction of the ship's interiors, will never forget the day that the walls melted. "To save money they decided to use raw vacuform sheets on the walls," he remembers. "They thought it seemed like a good idea as it was cheap, you could just throw it on, and it had a little texture to it. But when you heat it, it expands. So once the set was lit, it expanded and bubbled off! This was right before shooting. So we had to go to a day/night crew, 24 hours a day, to strip all that off and redo the walls. It was a total mess and a real nightmare."

"That was a good phone call to get," deadpans line producer Charles Newirth. "'The walls started melting...' That was a first. But that's the good thing about filmmaking – there was a fantastic art department and construction crew who spent the weekend pulling it off and then rebuilding it."

Thankfully, the remainder of the shoot proceeded without further melting-wall incidents. And if DeScenna was disappointed to lose the movie's original '60s look, she nevertheless created a distinct design that managed to feel sleek and modern while capturing the essence of the *Enterprise*. "When I was a kid I visited the set of the original *Star Trek* TV show," says the film's visual effects producer, Robert Stadd. "Linda's sets mirrored that feeling exactly. They were perfect."

The *Protector*'s bright, shiny, and blocky design sharply contrasted with the dank interiors of Sarris's ship. Mechanical effects supervisor Christian Colquhoun, who designed the cutting-edge mouthpiece inside Sarris's costume and operated his claw, says these crustacean-looking sets were both beautiful and very, very wet.

"There were lots of curves, with green and deep greens, and darker yellows," he recalls. "The main bridge was designed for simplicity and to emphasize the characters. When you watch, the control panels are almost like podiums, and they would underlight the faces of the characters. The design allowed you to easily see their reactions to anything happening. Lots of room for Sarris to pace around, walk from station to station, and stand over his lieutenants." Colquhoun adds that grates in the floor prevented it becoming slippery from accumulated water. "But it was dripping with water all the time, which compromised any foam latex appliances in use!"

EVOLVING CHARACTERS

The rehearsal time and the importance Parisot placed on perfecting character dynamics meant that the cast had already begun to gel by the time cameras rolled at the studio – once, that is, Alan Rickman adjusted to Tim Allen's unyielding commitment to making everyone laugh between takes. "There was fun to be had watching the chemistry between them on set," laughs Newirth. "Tim would come in and make fart noises and do outrageous, silly stuff. Alan would roll his eyes, and say [adopts Rickman's voice], 'Oh my god, Tim's doing this again. Can we just get to the acting?' Then you have Sigourney Weaver, who's in *Alien* for God's sake, one of the most iconic science fiction movies of all time. And Sammy Rockwell, who's fucking hilarious. So there were very different acting styles, but they all came together. The alchemy of those actors gave you the result of what you see on screen. That can't be replicated."

As the actors grew closer to their characters during production, they began adding little twists to their roles. Robert Gordon

Ve Neill applies makeup to Alan Rickman during one of the TV sequences. Left: Prop of the severed head of Sarris's lieutenant.

Prop: Profiles in History / www.profilesinhistory.com

remembers Alan Rickman as one of those who had a slightly different take on his part. "In the script I had written 'Sir Alexander Dane,' and Alan said, 'I'd like to remove the Sir.' I originally pictured Alexander as a great Shakespearean actor. But Alan played him as a sort of cut-rate Shakespearean actor. And I loved it. He was perfect! It's hard to see any other way of playing the character now."

In fact, all of the cast brought new dimensions to their characters, says Gordon. He recalls that Sam Rockwell gave Guy a "swagger" that wasn't in the script, while Sigourney Weaver imbued Gwen with genuine depth. "Gwen was not really a huge part, but Sigourney Weaver made it a lead part with her presence. I remember there were a bunch of takes for that 'I've got one job on this show!' scene. She started off kind of mild, and eventually went at it full-bore. She was always up for anything." Tim Allen, too, threw himself into his role, undergoing a rigorous training regime for the action sequences. He would later marry his personal trainer on the movie, Jane Hajduk.

Then there was Jed Rees, who played Teb. "His character was [originally] a nondescript Thermian, one of a bunch that I ended up combining. But he [Rees] took his character from a zero to a character who's the pilot of the ship at the end of the movie. I originally wrote it so the entire ship was going to land at the convention, but people convinced me that it was much too big to land there, so I wrote the ship separation. That meant that a lot of dominoes fell in such a nice way. Teb could now fly the ship, and Laliari and Fred could have that romance, which was something that Steven Spielberg wanted."

The romance between Fred and Laliari wasn't the only scene Gordon was asked to write at the last minute. He remembers one sequence that elaborated on Gwen and Jason's past relationship. "I was asked to write this, 'Hey, we've had our problems…' love scene, which happens in the midst of everything going on in the ship. But Dean and I had this shorthand if something wasn't working. He'd look over to me and make this scissors motion…" Sure enough, the scene never made it to the final edit. "The only thing I remember liking about that scene was the way it incorporated music from the [Galaxy Quest TV] show. I always thought the Thermians would add music from the show in different situations, but it was too complicated [to get across]."

As well as having to add scenes, Gordon and Parisot were asked to purge others entirely. Thankfully they held firm on story threads they believed in. "There were voices saying, 'You've got to cut the fans.' Thank goodness the fans stayed! I would have been so

MAKEUP MAESTROS

Galaxy Quest's three-time Oscar®-winning department head Ve Neill was, like many of the crew, well versed in *Star Trek*, having been a makeup artist on 1979's *Star Trek: The Motion Picture*. "I remember when I was reading the script to *Galaxy Quest*, I was just dying of laughter," she says. "I was beside myself, it made me so happy. It was so reminiscent of the old *Star Trek* shows. Fred Phillips, who did the original *Star Trek* series, was one of my mentors, and he asked me to do the first *Star Trek* movie with him... The makeup was still very heavy-handed back when we did that, and it was really kind of helpful for *Galaxy Quest*."

Neill's high-profile team included Bill Corso, who later won an Oscar® for *Lemony Snicket's A Series of Unfortunate Events*; Oscar® nominees Richard Snell (nominated for his work on *Star Trek VI: The Undiscovered Country*) and Hallie D'Amore (nominated for *Forrest Gump*); and Barney Burman, who won an Oscar® for his work on 2009's *Star Trek*. Burman recalls that he was largely tasked with making up background Thermians. "I applied their makeup to give them that blue-ish, pale look, and I made sure they weren't shiny," he says. "I also worked a couple of days helping Stan Winston's crew remove the alien makeup [from Robin Sachs]. I had to step out of the trailer so I wouldn't see them remove this 'secret device' that extended the actor's lip movements to the creature's lip movements – but it wasn't such a great secret!"

heartbroken. I mean, that was half of the movie to me."

Another of the studio's concerns was more understandable: namely that Parisot was planning to shoot in three different aspect ratios: the boxy 4:3 television aspect ratio for the TV sequences, the traditional movie aspect 1:85:1 for the opening scenes, and the Cinemascope 2:35:1 ratio for the moment the ship's doors open and Jason gazes out into space. "I always wanted it to change in scope because it's a love letter to filmmaking, but we probably overcomplicated it," Parisot admits. "The danger was when no one told the projectionists. They would open in 1:85 and then 10 minutes later they'd be projecting into the curtains! My very clever idea kind of backfired!"

Despite set-melting dramas and occasional creative differences (par for the course in moviemaking), almost everyone involved in *Galaxy Quest* cites the shoot as a career highlight. For executive producer Elizabeth Cantillon, it encapsulates a period in Hollywood moviemaking history that no longer exists. "This was a time when you watched dailies at the end of the day with the crew, which was really warm and fun," she says. "We wouldn't be able to make this movie here in town anymore because of tax incentives [elsewhere], but this was a real Hollywood production. It was a dream come true." ✦

Thermian performers are filmed on stage. They were composited into the viewing gallery of the starport as the *Protector* passes by.

GOBLIN VALLEY

The strange, beautiful Goblin Valley State Park was the perfect double for an alien planet –
but getting in costumes, beryllium spheres, and a full-size shuttle was a logistical challenge.

"**W**E WANTED SOMEWHERE DESERT-like and arid that felt otherworldly to represent the planet where they find beryllium," recalls line producer Charles Newirth. "And we knew we wanted to be in a natural environment, which was better for the actors to interact with. But it was tricky. Most places had already been used in other movies!"

Newirth joined location manager Liz Matthews and Dean Parisot in scouting various spots in New Mexico and Arizona. The task of finding somewhere where few films had gone before seemed hopeless, until Matthews hit upon the idea of Goblin Valley State Park in Utah, known for its towering rock pinnacles. "Those geological formations were very delicate, and they had never allowed filming there before," Newirth continues. "It was quite an accomplishment for us to get the government and National Park [Service] to allow us to film there."

Filming in the park meant that the cast and crew had to lodge in small motels next to a truck stop an hour's drive from the park – aside, that is, from Tim Allen and a few crew members, who stayed in motor homes on the park's outskirts. More of a logistical challenge

The cast film the sequence in which the heroes disembark from the surface pod. The full-size shuttle prop had to be taken in by helicopter.

Clockwise from top left: The rock formations known as hoodoos; light test with Sigourney Weaver; Parisot on location with his cast; the crew search for beryllium.

was the fact that vehicles – or anything on wheels – were not allowed to cross from the park's access road into the valley below. Bearing in mind that the shoot involved beryllium sphere props and a full-size shuttle amongst many other items, it didn't make life easy.

"We ended up hiring two massive cargo helicopters, which would airlift in our cameras, dollies, and cranes every morning and then get them out as the sun was going down," says Newirth. "It wasn't the kind of location where you could say, 'We'll pick up where we left off tomorrow.' We had to leave it clean every day. It was a monumentally difficult task."

Makeup department head Ve Neill remembers the time that key makeup artist Hallie D'Amore wrangled a mule to transport their equipment down into a valley – to no avail. "The park ranger came

out and said, '*What are you doing with that mule?*' They wouldn't let us take that down there either!"

The rugged terrain, costume-penetrating fine sand, and soaring temperatures only added to the sense of discomfort, not least because of the thick wool costumes. "It was really hot, which was kind of challenging, especially for Alan in that [latex fin] head," Neill says. "We couldn't even take tents out there, and there was little shade. We did what we could to keep everyone cool. Plus it wasn't easy to get alcohol, which didn't go down well with many people!"

"It was a challenge, but you can see the results in the film," says Newirth. "It was worth it. A lot of people looked at the movie and thought, 'Oh they did all that stuff digitally.' No, it's all real! It was so fantastic and unique." ✦

L.A. STORY

Locations in and around Los Angeles doubled for key settings,
such as Jason's luxurious home and the *Galaxy Quest* comic-con.

IN ADDITION TO ITS STUDIO LOCATIONS and the sojourn in Goblin Valley, the *Galaxy Quest* shoot took in various landmarks and residential dwellings around L.A., which doubled for some of the key locations.

Scenes at Jason's opulent home were filmed at Stahl House, a renowned midcentury modern house in the Hollywood Hills designed by architect Pierre Koenig. It wasn't the first or last movie to take advantage of the location's striking design, with Koenig's house appearing in everything from the rom-com *The Marrying Man* to Terrrence Malick's *Knight of Cups*. "It worked well because [Jason] had probably saved the most money out of the characters," says production designer Linda DeScenna. "I loved it because of the cantilevered, candlelit living room, and thought it would tie in with our [originally designed] late-1960s spaceship very well. Then that concept got kind of blown and we moved to *Buck Rogers*

[spaceship aesthetics], but we had already picked it [Stahl House] out. So I sort of felt that there was a disjointed look."

Gwen and Alexander's homes were filmed in less glitzy houses in residential areas of the city, as was the exterior of Brandon's house (scene of one of the greatest taking-out-the-trash moments in the history of cinema). "Designing [interiors to] the homes was fairly easy as I was a set decorator for so long," says DeScenna. "You just think about the character, the way they want him or her to come off, their income, what their life is like now."

Other filming locations utilized by the production team included the Santa Anita racetrack, doubling for the convention center car park where the fans guide the command module home (backgrounds of the center were composited in later); a parking garage at the Petersen Automotive Museum, which became the Tech Value Superstore; and the Hollywood Palladium on Sunset

A comic cover, illustrated by Warren Manser, used in the convention sequence; the cast and crew on set at the Hollywood Palladium.

Behind-the-scenes photo showing the full-size crashed command module at the convention. Inset: Two Galaxy Con banners, designed by ILM.

Boulevard, which was used to stage the *Galaxy Quest* convention.

The latter was a huge undertaking that required the art and props departments to generate a vast array of *Galaxy Quest* merchandise, from fake comics to T-shirts and tie-in toys of the *Protector*, nebulizers, and communicators. They may have only appeared on screen for a matter of seconds, but the props were lovingly created as if for a real convention. As well as *Galaxy Quest* merch, the convention scenes worked in displays from *Jurassic Park* (thanks to the involvement of Steven Spielberg and Stan Winston) and, sharing a stage with Guy near the start, a robot from 1992's *Toys* (which DeScenna had worked on). Many of the props were recreated in miniature by ILM, in equally loving detail, for the moment in which the command module crashes into the building.

The convention sequences also required the costume department to fabricate cosplay costumes for the attendees. These couldn't feel like movie studio costumes, but also couldn't look comically bad; rather they had to suggest the varying levels of quality that might be seen at a real convention. The costumes would also be used to suggest some of the wider characters in the TV show. "We bandied about a lot of ideas for the convention costumes," says Robert Q. Mathews, the costume supervisor charged with realizing costume designer Albert Wolsky's vision. "We knew we had to have something like the Klingons, Vulcans, and Romulans in *Star Trek*. I remember when we landed on the idea of the 'Fembots.' It was how they dressed on this all-girl planet on the show." Costume illustrator Gina DeDomenico worked up several cosplay designs, including the Mank'nar, an alien costume worn by several audience members and briefly glimpsed in a clip of the *Galaxy Quest* TV show.

Among the many extras at the convention was Robert Gordon, though his scene was sadly cut. "I was a [Dr. Lazarus] fan and Alan [Rickman] did my fin-head makeup," he says. "Dean panned by me as I was reading a *Galaxy Quest* TV script. It was so surreal. I mean, there were all these props and scripts for a television show that never existed! It was so much fun." ✦

Stahl House in Hollywood; Mank'nar illustration by Gina DeDomenico.

One of the Commander Peter Quincy Taggart headshots that Jason signs at the *Galaxy Quest* fan convention.

TIM ALLEN IS JASON NESMITH

As actor-turned-galactic hero Jason, Tim Allen showed a new side of himself in
Galaxy Quest. He talks science fiction, Yul Brynner, and kicking Sarris in the balls…

PERHAPS IT'S NOT SO HARD TO SEE why Harold Ramis couldn't picture Tim Allen as Jason Nesmith. Sure, Allen had proven himself a ratings winner on the small screen (*Home Improvement*) and big screen (*The Santa Clause*) alike. And, yes, he'd already lent his voice to one iconic spaceman in the form of Buzz Lightyear. But his resume wasn't exactly packed with action hero roles. And could he really pull off the story's more dramatic moments?

What Ramis didn't appreciate was how deeply Allen was into science fiction. From *Forbidden Planet* to *The Day the Earth Stood Still* (an original Gort prop sits in his office), he loved nothing better than a good space odyssey – and was thrilled at the prospect of starring in one. In fact, he was only too pleased when the comedy became less broad and the science fiction aspects were treated more reverently once Dean Parisot came aboard. "The movie took a decidedly different turn when they hired Dean," Allen says.

Allen adopted a stance borrowed from *The Ten Commandments*' Yul Brynner for moments in which he sat in the captain's chair.

"It became so much smarter because of Dean's point of view. He allowed the actors to play it as if it was actually happening. I love *Spaceballs*, but originally it was more like that: a much simpler comedy, a little more farcical."

Allen went on to head up a cast that largely arrived from a very different background than his own. With the exception of Daryl Mitchell, his other co-stars had honed their talents at drama school and the theater. Whereas they sat engaging in vocal exercises and the Meisner technique, he cracked jokes and made fart noises. It was a collision of two different worlds. "I'm in stand-up comedy, that's what I've done for 40 years," he says. "So when I go on movie sets, I don't sit and process like your contemporary actor processes. What I bring to it is that I'm a comedian. I'm basically a funny guy who says funny things. The challenge for me has always been sustaining any kind of seriousness. But if I get the chance and don't feel self-conscious about it… Deep as comics are able to go comedically, we are able to go dramatically."

Though Allen rarely abandoned his own cacophonous method of preparation, he took time to absorb the way his co-stars approached their craft. "I was around some very, very accomplished actors who I learned a load from," he says. Like them, he wanted to take his character seriously. After all, Jason was a role that involved more than saying funny things; as Robert Gordon has pointed out, Jason is essentially the "straight man" of the picture. Keen not to turn Jason into a simple Shatner pastiche, Allen looked beyond *Star Trek* to a classic Hollywood epic. "Odd as it sounds, I mimicked Yul Brynner in *The Ten Commandments*. The way that Yul Brynner sat there with his legs spread, his aggressive stance, his elbows – it [the performance] was that, it wasn't Shatner."

A dash of Captain Kirk was, however, channelled into Jason's alter ego, Commander Peter Quincy Taggart. "The only time I did Shatner was in those early TV series [clips], where he'd do those barrel rolls to get out of the way of alien gunfire… I mimicked him sometimes with his position. But we weren't making fun. I met Shatner because of this [movie]. He said he was a fan. It showed great respect for the fans and the genre, so how could [*Star Trek* actors] not like it?"

The movie showed Tim Allen could cut it as a dramatic actor and action hero as well as a comedian.

Tim Allen treated the film's science fiction elements with respect and tried to ensure that the story was as believable as possible.

CAPTAIN SENSIBLE

Allen's determination to take the science fiction aspects of *Galaxy Quest* seriously meant he had no truck with plot holes. Case in point: the moment the crew disembark from the surface pod after landing on the alien planet in search of a beryllium sphere. "In the script, we just got out of the shuttle. I was screaming at Dean, 'We can't just land the shuttle! We need to have some sort of device that tells us that there's oxygen!' Dean goes, 'Tim, I don't have any extra props. I don't have any choice.' Then Sam says, 'I'll do that.' And he says the exact same thing I was screaming at Dean – 'It's an alien planet! Is there air?'"

There were other times, too, when Allen channelled his inner Spock and questioned the logic of a situation, like the moment Jason loses his shirt in the one-sided fight against Gorignak. "I told them, 'Wait a minute. I can't do the rest of the show with my shirt off. That would just be weird.' Dean goes, 'Well, the [new] shirt's right there'. And we moved on. I'm the worst... Dean just stared at me half the time! But I love clarity of purpose, especially in science fiction stuff."

Another potentially great scene involving Jason was cut when Allen and Parisot realized they couldn't make it dramatically convincing. "There was a scene where I was supposed to knock Sarris down. But he was literally twice the size of me! I said to Dean, 'How is this supposed to work?' I suggested kicking him where his privates would be. In the scene [that was subsequently written], Sarris just stands there after I kick him, before lifting up a little panel on his chest and saying, 'Looking for these?' It was funny, but the scene went away

because there's no way I could hurt that creature."

Allen is keen to remind us that *Galaxy Quest* "isn't *War and Peace*." You never have to wait long for a belly laugh, and it's a movie expertly designed to leave you with a mile-wide grin on your face. But the dramatic moments are treated with integrity rather than a wink, never more so than when Jason admits to the tortured Mathesar that he and his colleagues are merely actors, that they "lied." It was the moment Allen proved to many he could cut it as a dramatic actor, and the scene earned (somewhat understated) acclaim from the top. "Spielberg, who happened to be on set, came by and said, 'Very traumatic. That was quite good, Tim.' Coming from Spielberg that was something." Nine years later, Allen went even further in proving his dramatic prowess playing a fading action star in *Redbelt*, which was written and directed by *Galaxy Quest* fan David Mamet.

Today, Allen understandably has much affection for *Galaxy Quest*, saying it's one of his films he will always watch to the end, whenever it's on. "It was such a good experience and far more than I had hoped. I had the same response [on first viewing it] that fans did."

Not only would Allen love to return to the world of *Galaxy Quest*, he has an irresistible idea for one possible plotline. "The Thermians return; because of lightspeed, it's been one year for them and about 15 years for us. And Sarris is back! When I see Sarris, I say, 'I thought you were dead.' He says, 'I'm not Sarris.' But he looks exactly like Sarris. He has the same voice. Then I say, 'I didn't know Sarris had a brother.' And he replies, 'I'm not his brother. I'm his sister…'" ✦

Sigourney Weaver underwent a makeover for the dual role of Gwen and Tawny, donning a blonde wig and fake breasts.

SIGOURNEY WEAVER IS GWEN DEMARCO

Sigourney Weaver explains the differences between Gwen and Ripley, and reveals why she felt like one of the Little Rascals on set.

YOU MIGHT ASSUME THAT SIGOURNEY Weaver's status as a bona fide science fiction icon would make her a shoo-in for the role of Gwen DeMarco and her karate-kicking alter ego, Tawny Madison. You would assume wrong. "It was a very strict rebuff when my agent called," Weaver remembers. "I said, 'That's ridiculous! It's those of us who have done science fiction that know how funny some of this stuff can be.'"

The initial decree that no one with the "baggage" of science fiction on their resume could join the cast was rescinded when Dean Parisot came onboard. Weaver's association with deep space – not to mention her box office clout – was now a definite asset rather than a distraction. But while the casting deftly played off her associations as Ellen Ripley, Weaver was clear from the start that this was a very different type of role, one she connected with on another level. "Ripley is not someone who imagines all the things that could go wrong – or she doesn't pay any attention to those voices. Whereas it was fun to play Gwen, who totally listens to all those voices about all the things that could go wrong. And it was an opportunity to play someone much closer to who I really am. I'm not a brave person who would be able to fight a monster out in space!"

For Weaver, the *Galaxy Quest* shoot was a period of nonstop laughter and unfettered joy.

Weaver saw Gwen as a tribute to the many beautiful actresses who arrive in L.A., decade after decade, determined to become big stars. "I feel like confident women come to Hollywood wanting to be the next Marilyn Monroe," she says. "Their confidence is eaten away by the competition and the rejection. That's why going out with the commander, who sent mixed messages, was actually very hard for someone like Gwen, who was such a nice person."

To make Gwen feel more like someone who aspired to be the next Marilyn Monroe, Weaver was adamant that the character had to be voluptuous and she had to be blonde. The studio wasn't so sure about the hair: they'd pictured Gwen as a brunette and weren't convinced that Weaver would look right as a blonde. To change their minds, makeup department head Ve Neill and head hairstylist Joy Zapata staged a test with the actress. "I appeared in costume before Steven Spielberg with my fantastic wig and huge bazooms," she laughs. "No one had really thought about who Gwen was, I don't think, and he was delighted."

For Weaver, the blonde wig and fake breasts weren't just window dressing. They were integral to showing how Gwen's appearance was linked to how she was perceived – and pigeonholed – in the world of show business. "I wanted to show how much courage it took to go anywhere with that body. I felt that Gwen had a very serious attitude toward the work and was devoted to being an actor, but because of how she looked and her measurements she wasn't taken seriously."

After a while, Weaver began to notice the effect that the wig and costume had on her. It wasn't all bad. "I think it brought out a more bubbly side of me, which surprised me, though it wasn't that hidden. And even I noticed that I had many more friends with that body. Everyone wanted to sit next to me at lunch. Between the blonde hair and the figure, I've never felt so popular."

BACK TO THE PAST

While the cast of the *Galaxy Quest* TV show are engulfed in petty resentments and internecine squabbling, the same was hardly true of the stars of the movie; you'll have to look elsewhere for stories of spectacular on-set falling outs. Like her co-stars, Weaver speaks of the shoot as a "joyous" time. "There was a lot of waiting around, as there often is on films with special effects involved, but Tim had us in stitches talking about who knows what. I often remember coming home hurting because I'd been laughing so hard. I think my funniest scenes were when we went back in the past [for the TV sequences]. Everyone had to have lifts and things like that to make us look

about 20 years younger for one day. It was impossible to look at anyone without shrieking with laughter. And I got to do some of my Tawny moves, which was very satisfying."

Things were no less joyous when the shoot moved from the studio to Goblin Valley, even if it felt as if she really *had* landed on a scorching desert planet. "It was summer and it was very hot. Our wonderful costume designer had put us in these wool uniforms because they looked the best in those conditions. But for me, wearing the fake boobs and the wig and the wool suit... I was constantly drinking to survive! But Goblin Valley was such a fantastic place and great fun when we were all together."

Then there was the climactic scene at the fan convention, shot at the Hollywood Palladium, which provided the perfect opportunity to stock up on unusual crockery. "That was my favorite part, I think. We roamed around seeing our faces on mugs and things like that. We were all trying to steal whatever we could. I still have a brilliant mug of Alan Rickman on one side doing some heroic pose and Tim on the other side, doing another pose. I also got a Tawny mug, which I keep in a very high cupboard because I don't want anyone to take it away."

The story dropped subtle hints about the backstory between Gwen and Jason.

Location filming in Goblin Valley was made challenging by the searing heat, which was compounded by the wig and costume.

RASCALS AT PLAY

Perhaps part of the reason the shoot was so much fun was the fact it rarely felt as if there was a studio breathing down the necks of the cast and crew. "It was one of those film experiences where you feel like the Little Rascals," Weaver recalls. "They [the studio] weren't looking on it as a great production that they were that excited about, so there wasn't a lot of supervision."

On the rare occasions that the studio did check up on the Rascals, however, they didn't always like everything they saw. Weaver recalls a "scary" read-through that led to Robert Gordon and Dean Parisot being issued with a ton of notes. "A lot of the character stuff that Bob had written – and Dean had completely wanted to do – that told you so much about each of the characters before we were in space went out the window. They basically said, 'We want them to be up in space right away.' That was a bit of a shock. Although in a sense, I think they were right because you still found out who we were in the course of the action."

Something that Weaver was less comfortable about being excised from the film were several of Alan Rickman's choice moments. "I was shocked and saddened to lose Alan's scenes, which I felt were the funniest in the script." And then there was the swearing, which was infamously cut or redubbed when the movie became a PG. "I lost some of my dirty, fun stuff with Tim," Weaver says. "And I had to say 'Screw this!' instead of, 'Fuck this!' [in the Chompers scene].

In the end it didn't matter – my whole body and soul were saying, 'Fuck this!'"

If losing the "Fuck this!" moment was disappointing, that was nothing compared to the way the movie was promoted. There were none of the international press junkets or prominent marketing campaigns that would usually be expected of a movie this size, Weaver remembers. "At the time, it was a little confusing why it wasn't made more of a big deal. I had never been in, or seen, a movie like this. We had total confidence in what we were doing. Bob wrote a great love letter to actors and what their belief in storytelling and each other can do... They didn't really see what they had, that's my opinion. They didn't understand that every single person who's ever watched anything like *Star Trek* would fall in love with this movie. It was frustrating because we had all worked so hard and so well together. But it's a film that has continued to charm people. So many people have come up to me and said it's their favorite movie."

Perhaps the greatest legacy of the shoot, though, was the fact it turned Sigourney Weaver into an unlikely rap star. As a birthday present for her agent, she dropped bars in her Gwen outfit alongside Daryl "Chill" Mitchell (who wrote the track) and Sam Rockwell. Missi Pyle and Patrick Breen were on obligatory dancing Thermian duties. "That was a highlight," she laughs. "Chill was so nice to come up with it and help me. I was 'Siggy Blonde Sig'... I know people who still call me that. It was the apex of my career, I think." ✦

Alexander Dane in character as the *Protector*'s science officer Dr. Lazarus.

ALAN RICKMAN IS ALEXANDER DANE

Alan Rickman's friends from the *Galaxy Quest* shoot
share their memories of the late, great actor...

DEAN PARISOT: Alan Rickman was the first person I went after. He was a brilliant actor in absolutely anything. His disdain is so funny.

ROBERT GORDON: From the time he was cast, I couldn't think of anybody else possibly playing him. He was so perfect. The first time I saw him, he was coming down the hallway, fresh out of a makeup test. He was wearing a white tank top and the fin headpiece, and he was grinning ear to ear. He was loving it so much. It was just the best way to see him.

JED REES: I had met him a year prior because I was doing a play in New York that his friend was involved in. After that, whenever I had auditions, I would ask him to run lines with me. Alan Rickman was coaching me for my audition! At the time, it just seemed like a natural thing to do. But in retrospect, it's like, *wow*.

TONY SHALHOUB: I had not worked with him before, although I had seen his work. I think I first became aware of him when I saw *Les Liaisons Dangereuses* on Broadway. I was a theater actor in New York, and remember sitting there and being completely

Rickman with Patrick Breen (Quellek). Years after the movie's release, the two actors would frequently attend each other's plays.

Dr. Lazarus defends himself from an alien attack in a sequence from the *Galaxy Quest* TV series.

bowled over. Watching him was kind of a revelation. I just remember thinking, 'Who is this man?' I wanted to explore everything he had done. I think I even went back to see that play a second time. So I was obviously an enormous devotee. And then to have the chance to work with him and become friends with him…

TIM ALLEN: I had a very separate upbringing to Alan. I would do fart jokes, screaming, just constantly making noise [before filming a take]. Alan would say, 'Can't you just be quiet before we start rolling?' He'd get so angry with me. I don't think he liked me. Then about three weeks into it, he came to dinner at my house. He brought a gift to dinner; I've never forgotten that. Elegant! He said, 'I've learned your process. Some of the great actors talk right up to camera to keep their focus away from overthinking the role. And that's what you do – because when you get to the role, you actually act very well. And your process is just as important as my process.' From that moment on, we became very good friends.

DARYL MITCHELL: I was a kid that came from the streets of rap, but Alan treated me like I went to Juilliard. When an extremely talented person lets you in like that and doesn't treat you differently, they put a level of expectation on you too… When you're working with someone like Alan Rickman, you have to *act*!

PATRICK BREEN: I remember the first time he saw the [Thermian] walk, it cracked him up. I loved making him laugh.

TONY SHALHOUB: In all of the times that I had watched him either in the theater or in film, I'd never really seen him let his hair down and get silly [before *Galaxy Quest*]. I think it was liberating and joyous for him.

SIGOURNEY WEAVER: The way he played his scenes was so marvelous and dry.

ENRICO COLANTONI: I can't say enough about Alan because he is the first actor I became friends with on a film set. I mean, intimacy happens very quickly on any film set, especially when it's an ensemble. But once the show's over, you usually sort of go your separate ways. I've never experienced a human being that really extended himself the way Alan did.

MISSI PYLE: Alan would eat with us every day. He'd grab his tray and come sit with us. It just felt normal and nice.

JEREMY HOWARD: Justin Long and I would sit right across from him and he'd regale us with stories of his work, the films he'd worked on, his acting tips. We constantly asked him questions because we were just starting out, and he was more than willing to offer up golden nuggets about acting. It was a special opportunity.

JUSTIN LONG: At the time, I thought it was special because I admired him – it was like, 'Oh cool, Alan's sharing his stories with us.' But in retrospect, I don't know if I appreciated just how cool and generous it was that this guy who had accomplished so much would sit with these kids who hadn't really done anything. That's a very rare thing for somebody at his level, but that's who Alan was. I don't think he gave himself that kind of status. He didn't have that value system. He just treated people equally and with respect. A lot of actors *say* they do that, but Alan really didn't value things like fame and status.

SAM ROCKWELL: Dear Alan Rickman became a very good friend of mine from that job. He was a mentor to me, and we talked about a lot of things. He later helped me with other things like *Charlie's Angels*. I remember Alan threw a 'mountain party' [party to celebrate reaching the halfway stage] in Largo [L.A. nightclub]. It was this great raving dance party! He was such a fun guy.

TONY SHALHOUB: Even after *Galaxy Quest* we stayed in touch. He would come see me in plays, and I would go to see every production in New York that he did.

ENRICO COLANTONI: My son and I visited him in London years later. I mean, how many people can say they got a tour of London with Alan Rickman as a tour guide? It was disarming, to say the least, how approachable and, dare I say, how ego-less he was. He just made room for you in his life.

MISSI PYLE: When I was in London, he was like, 'Come, let's go see a play together!'

PATRICK BREEN: He always came to plays that I was in, and I'd go see him do plays in New York and Dublin. I love Alan so much. I miss him.

DARYL MITCHELL: Alan invited me to his home in the country out there [in the UK] and I never got a chance to make it, which I feel bad about. I told him about my wheelchair, and he said, 'Don't you worry about that, we will take care of you.' I didn't know he was sick. Nobody knew he was sick, really.

VE NEILL: I actually have one of the photographs that we took of Alan on my desk so I get to see him every day. I worked with him again on *Sweeney Todd* and got to spend some nice time with him. He was such a lovely man and he is truly missed. And now I'm tearing up.

SIGOURNEY WEAVER: He was such a wonderful, wonderful man. So generous, so kind. Always this lucidity about what could help people and what was keeping them down and what our path should be to help make the world a better place. It was a great sorrow to lose him. ✦

Alan Rickman forged friendships with Tim Allen, Sigourney Weaver, and the rest of the cast during the shoot.

Tony Shalhoub played Fred as a serene, slightly out-there personality, who has a tendency to avoid reality.

TONY SHALHOUB IS
FRED KWAN

Tony Shalhoub looks back on the influence of cult 1970s adventure series *Kung Fu* and explains why much of his character's exploits were made up as they went along.

TONY SHALHOUB LOVED THE *GALAXY Quest* script. His agents loved the *Galaxy Quest* script. But something was holding him back. "It was a big-time commitment," he says. "And I wondered if it was the right project for me at that moment, which often happens." Shalhoub decided to ask someone whose opinion he valued to read the script and see if they thought he should take it on. "We were on vacation somewhere and I handed the script to my 10-year-old daughter, who was a really avid reader. I said, 'I don't know if this is necessarily a children's movie but tell me what you think of it.' She sat on a lounge chair by the pool and read it straight through. At the end she looked up at me and said, 'Dad, you *have* to do this!' I just trusted that. I'm still thankful to her because it pushed me over into making the decision."

Shalhoub initially met with Dean Parisot to discuss taking on the role of Guy Fleegman. Not long after, he received a phone call from the director informing him that Sam Rockwell had been cast as Guy, but asking if he would instead be interested in taking on the role of the insouciant, incessantly snacking thespian, Fred Kwan. Shalhoub had some reservations – or at least one reservation in particular. "In the script it's written as an Asian character, so I expressed some

Fred learns more about Sarris and the Omega 13 in the dining hall of the *Protector*.

One of Fred's big moments comes when he successfully operates the digital conveyor to bring Jason back on board.

bewilderment and concern there," he recalls. "Dean said, 'Let's not worry about it, we'll figure something out.' So then I said, 'Look, I won't play an Asian character but I'll play an actor who plays an Asian character.' So that's how it evolved. We had to rewrite and restructure the part as we went along."

For inspiration, Shalhoub and Parisot looked to the pilot of *Kung Fu*, the 1970s TV show in which David Carradine played the serene wandering monk, Kwai Chang Caine. Besides the show's character, they were influenced by behind-the-scenes gossip about the series. "The rumors in Hollywood were that Carradine really *was* stoned through most of the filming, which is how he was able to achieve such great stillness and that Zen quality," Shalhoub says. "So Dean and I had a conversation about that. And we also thought that maybe Fred was a bit of a burnout. We used that as the launchpad."

According to Sam Rockwell, Shalhoub also played the character as if he was a failed Scientologist. Shalhoub chuckles on hearing Rockwell's observation. "That was actually *Sam*'s idea that we adopted and adapted! I wasn't creative enough to come up with that on my own."

Aside from the changes to Fred's background ("Kwan's not even my real name!" the character exclaims at one point) and his blissed-out state, there was an even more last-minute change to the character when a romance was concocted between Fred and Laliari. Reportedly, the plot development came at the suggestion of executive producer Steven Spielberg. "I did not know that it came from Spielberg until later, but I thought it was a really good idea. I thought it was another way to connect these two species other than friendship and loyalty. Another avenue to explore. And, you know, Fred was sort of out-there anyway. He wasn't really fully human. So it wasn't that long a walk to imagine that [happening]!"

COLLISION OF STYLES

Shalhoub won plaudits from Parisot for the physical comedy he brought to the role (the director describes him as "almost like a silent comedian"), something Shalhoub says probably stems from his theater training. As part of the film's "theater contingent" – alongside Sigourney Weaver (whom he had known for many years), Sam Rockwell, and Alan Rickman – how did he find working with Tim Allen and Daryl Mitchell, who came to the film from very different backgrounds? "It was a very diverse group. And sometimes that doesn't gel. But in this case, there was a kind of magical osmosis. That's a tribute to Dean, I suppose, [who] facilitated all of these approaches working in synchronicity. In terms of Alan and Tim, they were on opposite ends of the spectrum in terms of their process. Yet it worked for the story really well because that was the reality of the *Galaxy Quest* series, where you had these different styles colliding. For me, the experience was joyous. I thought it was really fertile ground. It was creative, it was collaborative. And even though we all were sort of coming at it from different angles, there was a mutual respect and everyone was allowed freedom in the work."

Unlike his co-stars, Shalhoub largely escaped being thrown around by the set's giant gimbal. "My character was down in the belly of the beast, so thankfully I didn't have to get motion sickness," he points out. He also avoided the lengthy makeup work of his earlier science fiction comedy *Men in Black* (a franchise he would return to with the 2002 sequel, which was penned by *Galaxy Quest*'s screenwriter Robert Gordon). Nevertheless, he relished being part of a big science fiction picture surrounded by outlandish creatures, elaborate sets, and intricately designed tech. "It can be challenging in certain ways [working on a science fiction movie] because you have to be patient and sometimes defer to the technical aspects around you. But I love sci-fi and I like working within that [environment]. And what Dean did so successfully was the way [the film] wasn't a send-up, it was really a homage to the genre... He brought heart to it and walked the tightrope between genres."

Shalhoub drew on Parisot's genre-bending talents again just three years later – and the result was perhaps the actor's most famous role. "I knew that *Monk*, like *Galaxy Quest*, would require a certain tone. There was a balancing act between the comedy and the more poignant aspects of the script... I really believe that the success of the pilot and the way that [show] worked out was due to Dean's gentle touch."

Unlike Adrian Monk, Fred Kwan is a character who is seemingly free of fear ("That was a hell of a thing" is his reaction to the gelevator trip). But of course, Fred is more complex than he initially appears – witness the way he gains new confidence after he finally stops delegating and operates the digital conveyor himself, or ponder on his mysterious reasons for taking on a fake name.

Fred is so interesting and endearing that you can't help but want to see more of him in the movie. There would have been more, in fact, had two of the character's great scenes – one in which he rises dramatically to his feet in the mess hall before asking someone to pass the salt, and another in which he teases the answer about an unexplained proton surge out of Dian Bachar's nervous technician – not been snipped from the final cut. Shalhoub maintains a serene, almost Fred-like approach to the deleted scenes. "I felt that every character and every actor in the film was well served. Certainly, there have been other films where I pined for things that didn't make it, and others where I've been completely cut out. But in *Galaxy Quest*, I felt that whatever they did worked for the overall picture. It really wasn't about any one individual. It was about telling the larger story. And I'm so grateful to have been a part of it." ✦

A romance between Fred and Laliari was written on the suggestion of executive producer Steven Spielberg.

Guy's mustache and hairstyle were designed to make him appear older than Sam Rockwell actually was.

SAM ROCKWELL IS GUY FLEEGMAN

Sam Rockwell on how Bill Paxton, the Meisner technique, and gallons of coffee all helped Guy move beyond the role of Crewman Number Six.

B Y 1999, SAM ROCKWELL HAD A decade of movies behind him, including critically lauded indie dramas such as *Box of Moonlight* and *Lawn Dogs*. But he wasn't yet an A-lister with Oscar® prestige and a string of box-office triumphs to his name. Certainly, he wasn't the obvious choice for a big-budget science fiction comedy. Yet for casting director Debra Zane, he *was* the obvious choice. She was utterly convinced that Rockwell was right for the part

of *Galaxy Quest*'s nervy redshirt-without-the-red-shirt, Guy Fleegman. Less convinced, however, was Rockwell. "I turned it down a couple of times," he says. "I was supposed to do a lead in a Marisa Tomei time-travel movie that had been written for me [*Happy Accidents*], and I was really committed to that. And I didn't want to play a goofball or a coward. I didn't want to do comedies. I think I was taking myself way too seriously at the time!"

Sam Rockwell on location for the Tech Superstore sequence with camera operator William D. Barber.

Photo: Jeremy Howard

Rockwell changed his mind when he realized that prison drama *The Green Mile,* in which he played a psychotic convict, would hit cinemas the same month as *Galaxy Quest.* "The juxtaposition of the two characters was so extreme that actually I thought it would be a good thing to show range as an actor. And I remembered that [even] Sean Penn had done *Fast Times at Ridgemont High!*"

HIGH ANXIETY

It's a good job Rockwell changed his mind. The actor's nuanced take on Guy – who goes from oleaginous convention show host to terrified crew member to genuine hero – is one of the joys of the film, particularly the character's hilarious, wonderfully wired moments of high anxiety. Rockwell says there are shades of earlier screen portrayals of manic energy embedded in his performance. "I watched *Ghostbusters* and I watched Michael Keaton in *Night Shift,* which was helpful. Plus, Richard Pryor in *Stir Crazy* – his fear is very funny in that. You've got to steal from the best, you know? And I'm leaving out Bill Paxton in *Aliens.* The character was genuinely scared, but he was also the comic relief. I realized that was the function of my role. I kept asking Sigourney about Bill Paxton and eventually I think she got sick of me asking!"

For Guy's early scenes of unfettered eagerness ("Maybe I could sit in and, oh, sign a couple of autographs?"), Rockwell also drew on interviewees from the documentary *Trekkies,* part of Dean Parisot's "required viewing" list. Meanwhile, the character was made to feel a few years older than Rockwell actually was by the addition of a dashing mustache. (Rockwell would, after all, only have been 14 when Guy's lava monster episode is said to have aired in 1982 – though that's still five years older than nine-year-old pilot Laredo.)

The other key influence on his performance, Rockwell reveals, was a *lot* of caffeine. "I would drive myself crazy trying to get scared, because I didn't want to fake it. I treated it like a drama. I would genuinely try to get myself to the point where I was practically having a nervous breakdown. For that scene where I had to freak out as the shuttle came in to land on the desert planet, I had two Excedrin – which has caffeine in it – and three or four cups of coffee. I was losing my mind. I was a mess. I was constantly pacing around; I must have looked like a madman. In fact, when the scene was over, I had a hard time coming down and had to have a couple beers."

Caffeine come-downs were not the only on-set challenge. The sequence in which the pod gun-clutching Guy prepares to hold off Sarris's soldiers was difficult for a very different reason, with Rockwell revealing he shot the scene after just

Guy begins the movie as an unctuous convention show host who once had a small role on the *Galaxy Quest* TV show.

Sam Rockwell improvised parts of Guy's dialogue, including the classic line "Oh, that's not right!" as Fred and Laliari fall to the floor in an embrace.

finding out his grandmother had passed.

Other than that, he has nothing but positive memories of the shoot – and his cast-mates. Rockwell points out how important Weaver and Alan Rickman, in particular, were in helping him figure out his character. "Sigourney and Alan were mentors to me, and Dean gave them free rein to wrangle the actors. Sigourney and I would do repetition exercises – the Meisner technique, a listening exercise for actors. And Alan was like the captain. He got us together to read around the table and try to figure out things about the script – why we were there, what we were doing. It was really a team effort of actors dedicated to making a really great movie."

THE NEXT GHOSTBUSTERS

While Rockwell describes the script as "dynamite," his inventive ad-libs on the film ("That's not right!") had everyone in stitches. "There were always three takes for the director and one for Sam Rockwell," as tentacle puppeteer Christian Colquhoun recalls. Part of this was down to the collaborative atmosphere that Dean Parisot fostered on set, according to Rockwell. "Dean set such an amazing tone and made us feel so relaxed," he says. "I remember

when Sigourney's character had her zipper down to her cleavage, I said to Dean, 'Can you put me in a little two-shot with Sigourney? I think Guy should be checking out her bosoms.' I thought it would be interesting for the scene, and Dean and Sigourney liked that idea."

When Rockwell first watched the movie at its Hollywood premiere, he saw how the unwavering dedication of the cast and crew had paid off. "I thought it was fucking unbelievable," he says. "The audience just went bananas; I'll never forget it. I remember turning to someone like [then Warner Bros. President] Alan Horn and saying, 'This is the next *Ghostbusters*!' But then it didn't do as well as they wanted it to. Eventually, though, it became this beloved film, so my gut feeling that this was something special wasn't wrong. It just took time to gain credibility."

Rockwell calls the movie a "life-changing experience" and it's not hard to see why. It proved he could do big genre movies. It demonstrated his comic prowess. It kicked off lifelong friendships with actors like Justin Long. It showed he could pull off a mustache. And then, in between the endless cups of coffee, there was the revelation about English breakfast tea. "Sigourney introduced me to PG Tips!" he says. "Though I've since moved on to Yorkshire Gold…" ✦

Daryl "Chill" Mitchell as former child star Tommy Webber. In the original script, the Thermians still treated Tommy as if he were a child.

DARYL MITCHELL IS TOMMY WEBBER

The rapper-turned-actor reunited with *Home Fries* director
Dean Parisot for *Galaxy Quest* with hysterical results.

"I'M SO MAD THAT WE DIDN'T HAVE camera phones back then," says Daryl "Chill" Mitchell. "The real movie should have been about the making of [the film] *Galaxy Quest*! We had a party every day."

Mitchell's invitation to the *Galaxy Quest* party came from director Dean Parisot, who wanted to recapture the comic magic the actor brought to *Home Fries* – particularly his uniquely animated brand of rage ("Whenever he gets angry, it just cracks me up!" Parisot says). Tommy Webber had originally been written as an older character, but the part was rewritten for Mitchell, with *High School Musical*'s Corbin Bleu playing nine-year-old Tommy in the TV show sequences. "I felt comfortable and safe working with him [Parisot], and we had a great rapport," says Mitchell. "The rest is history."

Having played child navigator Lieutenant Laredo on the *Galaxy Quest* TV show, Tommy now had to learn how to pilot the ship for real.

Tommy heads to the *Protector*'s "media room" to pick up flying tips from his former show.

Mitchell admits he wasn't really familiar with *Star Trek* before taking on *Galaxy Quest*, but that changed during preproduction. As well as watching videos on comic-cons, he caught up on *Trek* and other classic science fiction. "It was great that I had come in blind. It wasn't like, 'Oh, I'm going to do what LeVar Burton did there.' But once I started watching these things, I couldn't stop. I got hooked."

If watching the shows was an eye-opener, that was nothing compared to strolling around the *Protector* set. "It was just like being at Universal Studios!" Mitchell laughs. "They'd created all these hallways, and then the [bridge of] the spaceship was built inside a steel frame on little pistons. We were *really* getting thrown around in that thing. One time it broke because it was shaking so hard."

SPARTACUS SPIRIT

Like Tim Allen, Mitchell didn't come from the drama school background of the rest of the cast, having made his name as part of the late-'80s rap group, Groove B, before appearing in comedy favorites such as *The John Larroquette Show* and *House Party*. He remembers his on-set preparation largely involved cracking as many jokes with Allen as humanly possible. "Alan Rickman had a process. Sigourney Weaver had a process. Over the course of time, after doing this for so long, I understand that now. But me and Tim… We would still be cracking jokes

five to eight seconds into them calling action! But that [difference of acting styles] is what made it work."

He remembers one particular long-running joke that irked Alan Rickman. "We had this thing where I would say, 'I'm Spartacus!' and Tim would say, 'No, I'm Spartacus!' And then I'd repeat, 'No, I'm Spartacus!'… I would try to catch Tim off-guard when he was somewhere else. But it didn't matter where he was on the stage – I'd say, 'I'm Spartacus!' and you'd hear him way off in the back saying, 'I'm Spartacus!' One day Alan was standing there when we were playing this and he said, 'Come on, let's get serious so we can get out of here, alright? Please.' We were like, 'Okay, Alan, cool, cool, cool.' So the next day we were waiting around for a second take on a scene. And out of nowhere Alan Rickman goes, 'I'm Spartacus!' He was like, 'Damn it!' Like, he didn't believe that had just come out of his mouth. He had just heard it so much, it had got into his head. All we could do was laugh and go, 'I'm Spartacus!' Oh man. We laughed for a good ten minutes!"

Aside from working with his co-stars for the first time, Mitchell also got to meet executive producer Steven Spielberg. Many people might be intimidated about coming face-to-face with Hollywood's most famous filmmaker – but not Mitchell. "When they introduced us to him, I said, 'Mr Spielberg, I would love to talk to you, but right now I am making a movie' – and he cracked up, man! [Another time] I came by and he was standing by the cooler, talking to the producer. I was like, 'Steve, can you pass me a water?' And he went down into the cooler, popped the top, and passed me the water without batting an eyelid or stopping his conversation. Everybody looked at me like, 'Yo, you didn't *really* do that, did you? Did you really ask the man to get you a water like he was a PA?' But that's how cool he was."

Despite all the on-set joke-cracking, Mitchell emphasizes that he took his character very seriously. "I wanted to keep the integrity and be true to the story and these characters," he says. He also points out that his background as a rap artist helped him connect to the themes of the movie. "In our rap music, man, we were the eyes and the ears of the community. When I was rapping, it wasn't about me, it was about *you*. Art is supposed to speak to people. And *Galaxy Quest* is a tribute to you, the audience, and the shows that preceded it. That's what we showed in the movie, too. Tim Allen's character [in the beginning] is like, 'Everything is about me. *I* gotta do this.' But then he learns it's about *us* and about his audience."

FAN FAVORITE

Like others in the cast and crew, Mitchell was disappointed at the time that the movie was toned down to achieve a PG rating (among other changes, Tommy's line, "You are so full of shit" was changed to "You're so full of it.") But he has come to embrace the decision. "I gotta say DreamWorks got it right. Adults loved it but children loved it even more. And people who watched it as a kid watch it again as an adult and still appreciate the movie."

Since *Galaxy Quest*, Mitchell has chalked up high-profile roles in shows such as *Ed*, *Fear the Walking Dead*, and *NCIS: New Orleans*, as well doing extensive work for spinal cord injury charities (the actor was paralyzed from the waist down after a motorcycle accident in 2001). But the fact that he nearly got the chance to return as Tommy in a shelved 2015 television series is something that still saddens him. "Don't break my heart, I would have loved to have done that, man. They would have had to work it out with my wheelchair, but I was coming back. I told my manager, I don't care what we have to do to make it happen. Because people love *Galaxy Quest*. On the set of *NCIS* people tell me all the time, 'I just watched *Galaxy Quest* again the other day!' I say, 'Let's have a *Galaxy Quest* party in the cafeteria.'"

Twenty years on, Mitchell is still having a *Galaxy Quest* party every day. ✦

Photo: Jeremy Howard

Top: The mining colony. Above: On location at the Petersen Automotive Museum.

CREW COSTUMES

Costume supervisor Robert Q. Mathews and costume illustrator Gina DeDomenico
reveal how they realized Albert Wolsky's vision for the crew's distinct outfits.

THE COSTUMES OF THE *PROTECTOR*'S hapless command crew and Thermian personnel wouldn't have been possible without dozens of textile artists, costume houses, stylists, and shoppers. But the concepts all began in the imagination of Oscar®-winning costume designer Albert Wolksy.

After studying the script and having discussions with Dean Parisot (and briefly, Harold Ramis), Wolsky became determined to create an interesting modern spin on the kind of costumes seen in *Star Trek*. One of his first steps was to get costume concept artist Gina DeDomenico (who, three years earlier, had worked on *Star Trek: First Contact*) to paint dozens of variations for the key bridge crew. "We tried all sorts of color stories with different seamlines, some with cap sleeves, some with stripes going down," DeDomenico remembers. "Sigourney's costume was especially fun. She'd been a badass in *Aliens*, but for this character we needed

The costume department used vintage wool to fabricate the command crew costumes, with additional pieces sourced from a century-old metalworking company.

THERMIANS

Tim Allen

Gina DeDomenico's costume illustrations for Jason Nesmith and the Thermians.

The Thermians' costumes were made from silver-plated fabric, while the TV costumes had to appear cheaper-looking than the crew's contemporary outfits.

to make her voluptuous and sexy. I drew the fake boobs with the zipper down the front and the long blonde hair, but we tried all sorts of hair colors. We pumped out a lot of variations for Sigourney and Tim Allen's costumes. Now, working digitally, I can create multiple color variations in a day. But back then you had to paint each one, so I'd paint a red costume one day, and blue the next!"

At the same time, Wolsky joined assistant costumer designer George L. Little and costume supervisor Robert Q. Mathews in scouring Los Angeles's boutiques to get an idea of potential materials. "We spent many, many weeks talking to textile artists and showing Albert what the possibilities were," says Mathews. "Over the course of that, Albert started working out the different ways he wanted to approach the characters."

OUT OF THE VAULT

When Wolsky spotted a vintage wool-knit fabric dating from the 1960s, he knew it was simply perfect for the retro look of the main crew costumes. Unfortunately, when the fabric house pulled out the rolls of material from their vault, it became clear the wool wasn't in great shape – not that it put Wolsky off. "There were moth holes in it, it was dated, and there was only a finite amount of the fabric," says Mathews. But, after dyeing the wool to obtain

the crew colors they wanted, it looked exactly like Wolsky had envisioned. Further modifications were made for the version of the uniforms glimpsed in the TV show in order to make them appear cheaper, including replacing the funky triangular zip pull tabs with a more standardized variety.

The costumes for both the command crew and Thermian personnel were matched with boots sourced from a vendor who made shoes for police departments, while collar pips denoting crew ranks were made by a century-old metalworking company. "George Little had worked on numerous military films, and knew military ranking and insignia like the back of his hand," Mathews recalls. "He set about figuring out the details of what insignia equals a captain, what equals a lieutenant, what equals a sergeant." As captain, Jason was also emblazoned with a series of crescent moons across his shoulders, a detail inspired by the shape of the *Protector*'s wings.

Although the crew costumes were perfect for the studio environment, the wardrobe department did encounter problems while shooting out in Goblin Valley – aside from costumes having to be helicoptered in because wheel racks were not allowed in the park. The woollen material proved uncomfortably hot in the arid environment, while the laceless boots were not well suited to the uneven, rocky terrain. "I had to go 45 minutes up a gravel road and then drive two hours to a shop that sold Dr. Scholl's [foot care] goodies," Mathews remembers. "I spent hundreds of dollars on stuff to put in their shoes to make them feel more comfortable!"

THE PEELING PLATES

As all Thermian culture is informed by *Galaxy Quest*, the aliens' costumes had to take a design influence from the TV show, while having a different, more otherwordly aspect all of their own. Before working up her illustrations, DeDomenico remembers Wolsky describing the Thermians' movements to her and specifying that her artwork needed to be "silver and shiny and kind of androgynous."

DeDomenico's approved illustrations were made a reality using a silver-plated fabric that was adorned with plastic shoulder inserts. Initially, the costume department intended to fabricate two or three costumes per actor, but they swiftly had to abandon that plan, according to Mathews. "In the course of filming, we found that while some people could wear a costume for a long time, other actors had something in their chemical makeup that would make them perspire more. The silver would start to peel away so you could see the fabric underneath! It wasn't unusual for us to go through a new costume in three or four days. I had to get the workroom at Bill Hargate [the designated costume house in Los Angeles] to keep churning them out."

The extra work was worth it. The dated but believably iconic outfits of the actors-turned-command crew and the shimmering Thermian costumes are, along with the department's Fatu-Krey costumes, testament to Wolsky's dedication to creating a distinct twist on science fiction concepts. "When I first saw *Galaxy Quest*, I was so thrilled and proud," says Mathews. "Albert had never worked in that realm [of science fiction] before. But he was always thinking about what had been done before, determining what not to do, and realizing the possibilities of what could be done in order to make the movie look unique. He achieved that a thousand percent." ✦

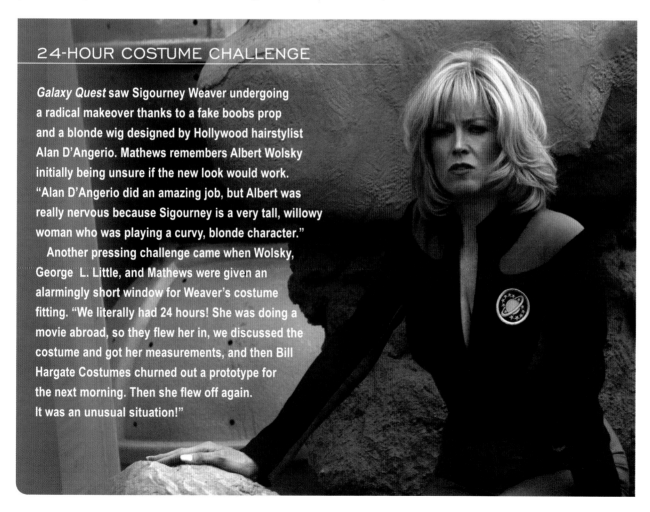

24-HOUR COSTUME CHALLENGE

Galaxy Quest saw Sigourney Weaver undergoing a radical makeover thanks to a fake boobs prop and a blonde wig designed by Hollywood hairstylist Alan D'Angerio. Mathews remembers Albert Wolsky initially being unsure if the new look would work. "Alan D'Angerio did an amazing job, but Albert was really nervous because Sigourney is a very tall, willowy woman who was playing a curvy, blonde character."

Another pressing challenge came when Wolsky, George L. Little, and Mathews were given an alarmingly short window for Weaver's costume fitting. "We literally had 24 hours! She was doing a movie abroad, so they flew her in, we discussed the costume and got her measurements, and then Bill Hargate Costumes churned out a prototype for the next morning. Then she flew off again. It was an unusual situation!"

THERMIAN CREW

The actors behind *Galaxy Quest*'s unwaveringly upbeat aliens share their memories of relearning how to walk and talk at Thermian School.

ALONGSIDE E.T. FROM *E.T.* AND THE Starman from *Starman*, the Thermians rank as some of the friendliest aliens ever seen in cinemas. Naïve, gentle, and infectiously optimistic, their admirable attributes are ruthlessly exploited by Sarris and the Fatu-Krey.

When it came to casting the key Thermians, Debra Zane and Dean Parisot found a disparate band of comic actors who all had unique takes on the endearing aliens. *Just Shoot Me!*'s Enrico Colantoni played lead Thermian Mathesar (initially known as Betzalar until the perceived similarity to *Coneheads*' Beldar

forced a Richard Matheson-inspired name change). The rest of the cast, however, was largely unknown at the time.

In addition to Missi Pyle, Patrick Breen, Jed Rees, and Rainn Wilson, other briefly seen Thermian actors include the late Sam Lloyd as Neru, Stan Winston's son, Matt Winston, as the lead technician who forgets to activate his appearance generator, and *BASEketball*'s Dian Bachar as an anxious technician (though the actor was virtually cut out from the movie completely). Many Thermians thrown around during the attack sequences were played by stunt performers.

Missi Pyle, Patrick Breen, Enrico Colantoni, and Jed Rees played the core Thermians. Attending Thermian School helped them refine the aliens' movements.

Mathesar, played by Enrico Colantoni, enjoys a Thermian beverage in the mess hall of the *Protector*. The character's voice was based on a theater vocal exercise.

MATHESAR (ENRICO COLANTONI)

Enrico Colantoni's initial audition went well. But while he'd succeeded in his aim of playing the character like "a Jehovah's Witness from space knocking at your door," he felt there was more he could bring to Mathesar (or Betzalar as he was then). He wanted to try a different approach – one he wasn't sure would be well received. "I said, 'Before I go, can I just try one more thing?'" Colantoni remembers. "And I did the vocals [like] it was a vocal exercise. It involves touching all the resonators with speech: the chest, throat, nasal, forehead, top of the head... It seemed to work. I was just being goofy, because when an actor plays an alien or a psychopath, you can't really be criticised toward its accuracy!" Suffice to say, the risk paid off: Dean Parisot and Debra Zane loved it.

While many involved in *Galaxy Quest*, from Parisot to the effects studios, were under the gun in terms of the schedule, Colantoni remembers the Thermian actors having considerable time to refine their roles at "Thermian School." It was testament to the importance that Parisot placed in character development. "I'd never been on a feature film that allowed rehearsal time like this. It was like theater school all over again, and it was hard not to bond because everyone was having so much fun. The school was set up so we could discover [Thermian culture] together and be on the same page –

though there were variations to the cadence or walk. Dean made it possible because he set the context. He didn't micromanage a single performance. He just let us play."

Colantoni went further than playing: he got to do some bona fide clowning. The actor had recently spent time working with the renowned Minneapolis theater company, Theatre de la Jeune Lune, where he had attended "clown class," and it was something that came in useful for the physicality of the role. "There was this clown aspect of the innocent Harlequin character... The kind of stuff that one usually isn't allowed to do on a film."

Colantoni's overriding memory of both rehearsals and shooting is of a "mosaic of talent and energy," in which everyone gelled. He credits Sigourney Weaver with holding everyone together and keeping them on track. "She was for all intents and purposes the *movie star* star, and she kept everybody calm. Tim would find an audience in a corner somewhere and start doing a routine, which would have everybody in stitches. Sigourney would gently tap him on the shoulder and say, 'Tim, come on. Time to go back to work...'"

On *Galaxy Quest*'s release, Colantoni's performance won praise from film critics and viewers alike – but it's the response from a friend he remembers best. "One friend who I respect very much left me a message saying, '*What the fuck was that?*' I could hear the smile on her face and knew it was the highest praise."

LALIARI (MISSI PYLE)

Jennifer Coolidge's audition for Laliari, in which she incorporated impressions of other "historical documents" that the character had absorbed, was a hoot. Yet somehow she wasn't quite right for the role. Enter Missi Pyle, three years out of drama school and with minor roles in *The Cottonwood* and *As Good As It Gets* to her name. "I went to see Debbie Zane and she said, 'I don't normally do this, but I'm going to show you another actor's audition so you can get the tone, because we're having a hard time.' And they showed me Jed Rees auditioning for Enrico's part. I watched the tape and was like, OK, I know what to do with this. I know who they are. They're like children. They're smart but also naïve. And they can't understand anything other than being nice. I also thought about watching my mom on stage in choir as a kid and how happy she seemed to be up there."

To Zane's relief, it was clear from watching Pyle's subsequent audition that they had finally found what they were looking for. "Debbie told me that she took a photocopy of her CSA [Casting Society of America] card, put it on my audition [tape] and said to Dean, 'I will quit the union if you don't hire her.' It was one of the nicest things."

Thankfully, Zane wasn't required to quit the union. Pyle won the role, and she immediately began work on refining Laliari's movements and personality, as well as thinking about how she fitted into the wider Thermian culture. "I had a yellow notepad to take notes on what these characters were like. We had different ideas. I [initially] had an idea that they would just fall over sometimes because they didn't know what they were doing. Then we came up with the idea of them getting a little too close [to other people], because they didn't understand personal space. And Enrico set the tone of how they would talk."

Pyle is unique in that she gets to speak "real" Thermian in the movie. Where did that shriek come from? "It said in the script it sounded 'like a screaming baby in a bagpipe,' which I thought was so funny. You know, I just tried to make it sound like baby brokenness!" Pyle duly launches into Laliari's Thermian screech, which is just as demented and funny and terrifying 20 years on.

While some actors like Rainn Wilson and Dian Bachar saw their roles diminish during production, Pyle's character was actually made more prominent. First she replaced Susan Egan as the hologram who invites the cast to step onto the gelevator discs. Then the romance with Fred was introduced at Spielberg's suggestion. "I remember my makeup artist, Bill Corso, told me that Spielberg had seen my tape and wanted to expand it," she remembers. "That *never* happens!"

The role of Laliari was expanded to include a romance with Fred.

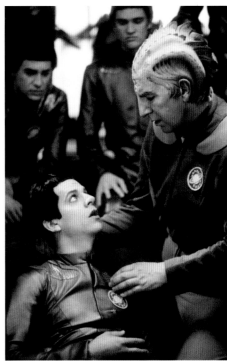

Patrick Breen shared several scenes with Alan Rickman, including the moment when Quellek dies in Alexander's arms.

QUELLEK (PATRICK BREEN)

We might have Gerry Anderson to thank for the Thermians' distinct movements. It was during a "cultural rehearsal" with his fellow Thermians that Patrick Breen had a vision of Anderson's beloved Supermarionation productions. "When puppeteering a marionette, you can't get them to walk the way normal people walk," he says. "It was always the same opposite arm and opposite leg swinging when they walked around. So I said to Dean, 'What if they walked like that because they've watched *Thunderbirds*?' He said, 'Oh yeah, we're doing that!'"

However, Breen remembers it took time to master the Thermians' puppetlike movements. "It was pretty difficult because it takes a certain amount of coordination to unlearn how to walk. And then the poor extras who were in every scene... watching them struggle with walking in the background is something I enjoy when watching the movie!"

For Breen, Thermian School was the perfect opportunity to build a sense of unity between the characters without stifling the actors' individual approaches. "It was so goofy and they had hired really terrific comedians to play the parts," he says. "We all got along. Debbie and Dean were just really intuitive [in the casting process]."

Breen says that along with marionette movements, he took a flavor of Colantoni's vocals and gestures, and fashioned a character, akin to a wide-eyed adolescent, who literally wasn't comfortable in his own body. "We're cephalopods, so we're not quite used to being in these bodies, even using the image generators. So there's an awkwardness of speech and awkwardness of movement, and certainly an awkwardness of emotion."

Quellek emerges as a fanboy to rival Brandon in his worship of Dr. Lazarus – something Lazarus/Dane is disdainful of, until the Thermian's moving death scene. Was that sequence as emotional to shoot as it was to watch? "Nobody was talking or joking as we clearly wanted to continue to feel that way until we'd finished the scene," he says. "I remember we shot Alan's coverage first, with me in his arms. Then we turned the camera around and did my coverage. I just thought, 'I know it's a comedy, but let's play it for real...' You know, he would just be so moved to have Dr. Lazarus there. Maybe I sank into it a bit more on my coverage, as Alan actually asked to reshoot his coverage after watching my take on it to match what I had done. It was so lovely that he suggested that and that Dean agreed. Then he played it the way he did in the movie – really grounded and very heartfelt. It was a gift to Quellek."

Above left: The pig lizard-splattered Teb in the digital conveyor room with the command crew. Center: Teb, Mathesar, Laliari, and Lahnk at the fan convention.

TEB (JED REES)

After many years working in his hometown of Vancouver, Jed Rees drove his beat-up car to Los Angeles to try to make it in Hollywood. As luck would have it, the first script that came his way on arrival was *Galaxy Quest*. The fact that he had previously worked with both Debra Zane and Dean Parisot (the latter on an episode of *The Marshal*, where he played the not-career-defining role of 'Man in a hot dog outfit') helped him get a shot at an audition for Mathesar. "The inner pull to go to L.A. was very strong, and I always thought there was a bit of magic involved as far as everything lining up," he says.

While the role of Mathesar went to Colantoni, Rees was cast as the irrepressible Teb. Rees remembers Teb's character outline describing the Thermians as "Disneyland employees who can't fathom lies," and he began trying to get into the mindset of what that might feel like. "I thought there was a certain Christianlike quality to them – that positivity. There was also a nonjudgmental quality I wanted to interject. Then I imagined that they might have learned to talk using some sort of phonetics document, which made the way they spoke almost perfect in a certain way."

However, Rees wanted Teb to be more than a one-note, relentlessly happy character. After all, this is someone who has seen his homeworld decimated and his species almost wiped out. "I figured that on the outside he's very happy, but on the inside he is terrified that all of his people are going to be destroyed. Having that juxtaposition and conflict inside the character was fun for me."

Rees is also surely one of the few actors to be influenced by Glen A. Larson's superhero drama *NightMan* – or at least by his own performance on that show. "I played the henchman, who was much like a butler, to an evil guy played by Kim Coates. I definitely brought a few elements of the way I played him into Teb."

Rees has nothing but fond memories of working with his co-stars, from the Thermians ("If I run into any of those guys now, there's still a total love and a total bond") to the command crew ("I was pretty fresh as an actor and I was watching everybody to see what their process was"). But he admits that acting alongside so many big names was initially a nerve-wracking experience. "The first scene I shot was where Teb explained the food to the *Galaxy Quest* guys. Here I am, delivering a speech to Sigourney Weaver, Alan Rickman, Tim Allen... My stomach hurt so bad from nerves." They weren't the only famous actors Rees saw during the production. "I was smoking a cigarette with Rainn Wilson outside, dressed in our alien costumes and itchy wigs. Then Jack Lemmon rode by on a golf cart. He just turned to us with this look of '*What is this?*'"

Above right: Lahnk, Mathesar, and Laliari arrive at the door of Jason's house doing the *Galaxy Quest* salute.

LAHNK (RAINN WILSON)

Six years before playing one of America's most popular sitcom characters in the form of *The Office*'s Dwight Schrute, Rainn Wilson made his movie debut as Lahnk in *Galaxy Quest*. In many ways, it was a role tailor-made for Wilson's personality. "Acting like an alien was very easy for me because I had been doing it since I was four years old," he says. "I guess I was sufficiently alienlike to be cast. And I was a big Trekkie from early childhood... I just loved the way that it played with it [*Star Trek* concepts]."

Viewers will notice that Lahnk disappears midway through the movie, which was down to the fact that Wilson had to depart the set for a TV pilot. "The show was called *The Expendables*. Not the action franchise with Sylvester Stallone playing an old person. This was about naked, indestructible androids. It was one of the worst TV pilots of all time. The Thermians would have loved it."

Still, Wilson did get to appear in a handful of early scenes, and as an added bonus he got to enjoy an on-set sauna. "The spacesuits fitted my body perfectly and I was very excited. But an hour after putting it on, I realized the amount of sweat coursing off of my body while wearing said uniform was just preposterous. The sweat would pour out of my body, down into my underwear, and into my socks."

Sadly, Wilson's biggest scene, in which he informs Fred about unexplained proton charges, was cut completely – something that came as a surprise. "I went to the cast and crew screening and no one had let me know. It was really disappointing."

Yet he admits he can see why the sequence might have been cut. "There was a lot of technical jargon that I thought I had memorized. I went over it the night before and the morning as I was driving in. But all of a sudden, we got to the rehearsal and I was like, 'Holy shit, this is impossible! It's like memorizing random phonetic syllables!' And I was nervous – it was my first movie, there were all of these big stars lined up behind me, and I had this paragraph of jargon. When you view it on the deleted scenes on YouTube, you can see the panic in my face as I'm trying to get the line out. You see some kind of stutter, you can see I'm really struggling with it. It was the actor's nightmare come to life."

At least with the scene cut, he doesn't have to relive the experience every time he watches the movie – which is regularly. "I've seen it six or seven time and my son's seen it four times. It's one of those rare classics. It would never get the green light today – they don't really make movies in that budget range any more. But it's an absolutely pitch-perfect film." ✦

THE FAN CLUB

Justin Long channelled both his nerves and the spirit of his screen
heroes to play Brandon – the authoritative fanboy turned hero.

IN MANY WAYS THEY'RE THE REAL heroes of *Galaxy Quest*: the band of unwavering fans, led by Justin Long's Brandon, whose encyclopedic knowledge of the show helps them direct Jason and Gwen through the Chompers and guide the crew back to Earth.

Behind the scenes, Long was on something of an adventure himself. *Galaxy Quest* marked the big screen debut of the then 21-year-old actor, and as a huge movie fan he was thrilled to recognize famous names such as Tom Everett Scott, Eddie Kaye Thomas, and Kieran Culkin at the casting office before he'd even got the part. But he also vividly recalls how anxious he felt at that first audition. "I was intimidated and so nervous," he says. "But I think that lent itself to my audition and to my performance. I mean, the stakes were so high for me, as they were for my character. I just had this natural nervousness that I was able to lean into."

The movie nerd in Long only became more excited – and more nervous – when filming began. Not only did he relish classic Hollywood sights like alien-suited extras sucking cigarettes on the lot in between takes, but he found himself working with household names such as Sigourney Weaver and Alan Rickman. "I was a huge *Seinfeld* fan and I remember getting my picture taken with Heidi Swedberg, who played my mom!" he laughs. "I remember there being a real fear that now that I was playing alongside these professionals, I didn't want to be caught having a false moment. I just wanted to be as present and as truthful and as authentic as possible."

Sometimes he took this fear of not being truthful a little *too* far. "It was my first day of shooting, and I was really hung up on the reality of that model airplane I was working on in Brandon's bedroom. The camera guys would say, 'Can you look over here?' and I remembering thinking, 'But if I do that, I'm not going to be able to look at the pieces I'm working on!' The pieces, as it turned out, didn't really matter. But it worried me to fake something.

The fans guide the command module home using Roman candles. The scene was shot at Santa Anita racetrack, with the background digitally inserted in post.

Brandon (Justin Long) at the convention center with fellow "Questarians" Kyle (Jeremy Howard), Hollister (Jonathan Feyer), and Katelyn (Kaitlin Cullum).

I'd only really done theater where everyone could see what you were doing. I had no conception that the camera was only concerned about certain things."

Sometimes, others would take advantage of Long's naïveté about the movie business. He chuckles at remembering a conversation with a background performer in the climactic sequence at the convention center. "It was a crane shot following me and my friends through the crowd. There was a lot going on – smoke, special effects, bricks being thrown by props people – and Dean had told me the path I was to take through the crowd. Right before we did the take, one of the background actors nervously approached me and said, 'What if we do a high-five like we're friends as you pass me?' I went, 'Yeah, OK, I can do that.' Because I thought it was collaborative! Other background actors saw that and descended on me and were like, 'How about we do something too?' Suddenly I was trying to keep track of all this business I had to do as I'm running through. Then when they called 'Action!', I was doing a high-five with one person, a wink with another, an 'Ooh' with another – and it took me a long time to get up to my mark. Dean, slightly frustrated, said 'Justin, *what are you doing?* What's all this stuff?' I was like, 'Oh, we had this thing worked out...' I turned around and the [extras] were gone! They'd just wanted to have a thing in the movie. But as Alan would have said, I needed to be present in the

reality of that scene. This ship had just crashed and my character's intention should have been to get to the stage as quickly as possible to see if his friends were alive! It was an important lesson for me."

COMIC INFLUENCES

As well as channelling his genuine nerves, Long drew on several of his comic heroes for the character. This included Chris Farley ("especially the hero worship [in *Saturday Night Live*] when Farley sits down with Paul McCartney and is like, 'Remember when you were in The Beatles?"), Michael J. Fox ("I just love his cadence and his delivery"), and Philip Seymour Hoffman ("specifically Phil in *Boogie Nights*"). Long actually got to meet the latter when he paid a visit to the *Galaxy Quest* set one day. "It was such a thrill. I was so starstruck! We all went to see *Deep Blue Sea* at the ArcLight after shooting. When Samuel L. Jackson gave that over-the-top speech before being eaten by a big, obviously CG shark, Phil was howling with laughter. That set Tim Allen off. It was so entertaining just watching the two of them!"

The Simpsons' Comic Book Guy was another influence, largely on Brandon's more arrogant side. "Brandon is the authority figure in his little circle, and there's no better example of that than Comic Book Guy. Like when he's asking that question to Tim Allen at the convention... his power is what he knows." But even with Comic

Brandon assists the *Protector* from his bedroom. Long says he was struck by the attention to detail of the production design.

Book Guy at the front of his mind, Long remembers that early in the shoot he was worried about being "over-zealous" in his performance. That fear was allayed when Dean Parisot gave him a copy of the 1997 documentary *Trekkies.* As he watched the video in his hotel room that night, it struck him that he wasn't going too over-the-top. Far from it. "I realized there are people who *are* that zealous about *Star Trek* and fandom. I hadn't really experienced that type of person. And there was one interviewee [Gabriel Koerner] in it that was kind of like Brandon… it was helpful to watch the kid in that movie because he was obviously so sincere. That was the key to the character: committing to the sincerity of it and not playing any sort of affectation. An important part of Dean's direction was that he really respected these characters and the multidimensionality of them."

Thanks to Long's believable take on the character, Brandon emerged as integral to the story's heart, while being the source of some of the film's funniest sequences (though Long remembers that one of his best moments – Brandon taking out the trash as the *Protector*'s self-destruct sequence counts down – was in danger of being cut at one point). Watching the film and his performance for the first time at the premiere, Long felt an overwhelming sense of relief. "I remember thinking, 'I didn't stand out as being bad. I didn't ruin anything!' And it was exciting to be part of something that was good. I sometimes cringe a bit watching my old performances, but I don't get that with *Galaxy Quest.* Although years after the film, I saw a photo of the leather jacket I wore to the premiere… *that* was embarrassing. I thought I looked so cool!"

Twenty years on, the film has built up a fandom worthy of Brandon and his gang. So why does Long think the film – and his character

– has endured? "There's an innocence to the fans that is very charming," he says. "And it's a very sincere and relatable film about truth and friendship that you don't see in many comedies. Like when Patrick Breen's character is dying… if the orchestra had swelled a little more or if Alan Rickman had shed a tear, it might have crossed the line into sentimentality. Yet it managed to pull off that high-wire act, that delicate balance. There's a real human quality to it." ✦

Justin Long on set with Missi Pyle for the Tech Superstore sequence.

Photo: Jeremy Howard

KYLE: BRANDON'S BUDDY

Kyle, the world's number one authority on the *Protector*'s utility tunnel system, was played by the then 18-year-old Jeremy Howard. The actor initially auditioned for the role of Brandon. While he didn't get the part, casting director Debra Zane loved his take on the character so much she cast him as Brandon's equally obsessive buddy.

Though *Galaxy Quest* was not Howard's first film (he had small parts in the 1995 weepie, *The Cure,* and the true-life TV movie, *Crash Landing: The Rescue of Flight 232* – the latter scripted by Harve Bennett, writer of *Star Trek II, III,* and *V*), it was his first experience of being surrounded by huge sets and A-list actors. "It was so amazing, but when you start out you think, 'Oh, it's *always* going to be like this – I'll always get to go to sets and work with an amazingly talented cast and crew who are super nice and funny,'" he says. "It's too bad I was 18 and didn't realize how rare that is. Everything was so perfect on that set that it spoiled me."

Howard spent six weeks on the movie, and he remembers being in awe about the little details of the shoot, whether it was the *Jurassic Park* display at the convention ("Since Stan Winston and Spielberg did it, they used two of the original velociraptors, which I thought was the coolest thing ever") to Tim Allen's array

of supercars ("He seemed to show up in a different one each day.") One of his favorite memories is the time he introduced his parents to Sigourney Weaver. "My dad was a *huge* fan of *Aliens.* And when my parents came to visit the set at the Hollywood Palladium, she chatted to them about acting and life for, like, 30 minutes, and even invited them to her trailer. She was one of the kindest, sweetest people I've ever met."

Despite the joyful shoot, the experience of watching the movie for the first time was not without disappointment. Two of his sequences were cut: the first in which Kyle and his fellow fans sit in a cardboard cut-out spaceship waiting for Jason to show up; the second in which Kyle is revealed to be downloading porn while studying graphs in his bedroom. "I remember getting a big laugh out of the video village for that porn bit. But when it became a PG, that was cut. The coyness of my line reading was a set-up for that comedic reveal – I'd have done it differently had I known! I remember being so bummed those bits were edited out that I didn't really absorb the fact I was watching such a brilliant movie until the second time I saw it. Thankfully with age, that 'young performer' ego melts away and you realize what an honor it is to be a part of a project like *Galaxy Quest* at all!"

These days Howard is a veteran guest of comic-cons himself, thanks to his role as Donatello in the 2014 and 2016 *Teenage Mutant Ninja Turtles* movies. But *Galaxy Quest* remains one of his favorite projects. "It's a film that doesn't make fun of fans and it really speaks to people. There isn't another movie like it."

Photo: Byron Purvis/Admedia/Jeremy Howard

Photos: Jeremy Howard

Zieliński and Parisot shoot the Tech Value Superstore scenes at the Petersen Automotive Museum. Photo: Jeremy Howard

SHOOTING STAR

Cinematographer Jerzy Zieliński on the influence of *2001*, shooting
the film as a drama, and his ceaseless battle against the gray.

DREADED COLOR APPEARS BEFORE cinematographer Jerzy Zieliński's eyes every time he thinks back to *Galaxy Quest*. "The gray!" he says with a shudder. "There was a gray starship with miles and miles of gray corridors and gray glass walls. The costumes of the aliens were grayish. I was in a gray world – and at that time, gray was the most difficult color to be photographed!"

Zieliński was brought onto the film by Dean Parisot just four weeks before shooting. The fact that Zieliński and Parisot had previously worked together on *Home Fries* and *A.T.F.* meant they

had already established a strong working relationship, but that didn't lessen the challenge of figuring out how best to shoot the movie with so little time to prep.

"Some of the sets had already been built," Zieliński recalls. "But because the starship in the story had been built by aliens based on a crappy TV show, the sets weren't loaded with the usual sci-fi elements. It was tricky to make it work visually." A 30-year-old science fiction classic helped unlock that visual style. "On reading the script and seeing the sets, I realized the style was closer to *2001: A Space Odyssey* rather than, for example, *Alien. Alien* used

The interiors of the *Protector* were clean, gray, and flat, which contrasted with Sarris's grimy, yellowish-green starship.

a lot of smoke and vapor and different light sources, but *2001* had flatter walls and a cleanness to it. The humor of *Galaxy Quest* played better in cleanly lit environments."

Though the tone of *Galaxy Quest* was clearly very different from *2001*, Zieliński never dwelled on the fact he was filming a comedy. "Dean told me to shoot it like a drama, rather than think of comedic camera angles. Shooting it straight made it funnier."

TESTING TIMES

To figure out the best way to light and shoot the film, Zieliński conducted a large number of tests in the ultra-short timeframe. "I tested [how lighting affected] the costumes, the makeup, skin tones, as well as the temperature of the lights." These tests often involved working closely with other departments as the VFX, costume design, and production design all had a big impact on the lighting.

Testing and planning were particularly important, says Zieliński, because of the technical limitations of the period. "Today you can do a lot more things in the color correction process, like fixing parts of the frame, especially if you're shooting on digital. But back then, if you made a mistake and tried to fix it in color correction, it might have an impact on the skin tone. You had to live with mistakes."

To bring the interior of the *Protector* to life, Zieliński and his team inserted a large number of LED light strips into small openings in the ceilings of the set, compensating for both the gray and the demands of anamorphic lenses. The latter required a high amount of light to be pumped in – something that didn't react well with the mylar floors and vacuform walls, which melted during one test.

The monochrome of the starship was, in fact, just one of the three color palettes in the film, says Zieliński. "Sarris's ship was a kind

of rotting yellowish-green. And the desert was warm and kind of orangey. Luckily, there was no drastic change of weather when we shot in Goblin Valley – it was much less challenging, say, than one film I shot in Ireland [1984's *Cal*], where there was sun, cloud, and rain all in the same day!"

For the *Galaxy Quest* TV show, which was filmed in 4:3 aspect ratio, Zieliński took a slightly different approach. "It had to be shot like a TV show in the 1970s – much more awkward. Too many lights, too many shadows, too many colors."

Zieliński ultimately succeeded in his battle against the gray, and it remains one of the highlights of the cinematographer's career. "It was a challenge, but we had a great crew and Dean is a very good director," he says. "The film has not really aged at all, and I still like watching it – that's not true of every film I've worked on." ✦

Jerzy Zieliński today. The cinematographer also worked on Parisot's *Home Fries*.

Tawny high-kicks an assailant in a sequence from the *Galaxy Quest* TV show. The TV scenes required Armstrong to coordinate stunts that were more absurd and mistimed.

ACTION STATIONS

Stunt coordinator Andy Armstrong looks back on blowing up spaceships, smashing apart corridors, and splattering bad guys against windscreens.

I T WAS 1976 – AND STUNTMAN ANDY Armstrong was at Pinewood Studios in the UK, working on offbeat spy romp *The New Avengers*. In between takes, he would wander over to watch *Space 1999* being shot on the stage next door. "I remember seeing extras walking around with these grille-like tanks on their back," he says. "When I looked carefully, I realized they were just draining boards that you put your dishes in! It was kind of ridiculous and wonderful."

Thankfully, *Space 1999*'s prediction of the moon being knocked out of orbit during its titular year never materialized. What did materialize in 1999 was something perhaps equally historic: the filming of *Galaxy Quest*. During the shoot, Armstrong – by now a veteran stunt coordinator – regaled Dean Parisot and others with his

memories of Gerry Anderson's beloved sci-fi drama. "*Galaxy Quest* tips its hat perfectly to shows like *Space 1999*, especially in the TV series you see in the film," Armstrong says. "We had to design action for the [*Galaxy Quest*] TV show that was a little out of sync like in those old shows. The bullet hits went off a couple of seconds before the gunfire, things like that. It was difficult at first – we had to keep changing the timing of everything as we couldn't make it look absurd enough!"

There is, of course, much absurdity in *Galaxy Quest*, but Armstrong points out that his approach as stunt coordinator was to treat the real-life action scenes as seriously as possible. "Dean and I felt we needed to play the action absolutely straight, as if we were making an action movie or a war movie. The humor needed

Andy Armstrong (center) on set with VFX coordinator Amanda Montgomery, second assistant director Phil Dupont, and VFX supervisor Bill George.

Clockwise from top left: A Fatu-Krey guard is splattered on the *Falcon*'s viewscreen; stunt double John Casino lands a punch; Tim Allen watches Andy Armstrong and Stan Winston demonstrate the strength of the jacket that Jason and the pig lizard tussle over; Armstrong oversees the rolling of a beryllium sphere.

to come out of the setup and the ridiculousness of situations rather than the action itself."

An example of this is the sequence in which one of Sarris's guards is ejected from the airlock of the *Protector* and splatters over the viewport of Sarris's ship – a very funny gag that looks completely realistic. "We put a stunt guy called Tanner Gill on a fan descender device, and then dropped him at almost freefall speed towards a big piece of Lexan that replicated the window," laughs Armstrong. "[Special effects supervisor] Matt Sweeney gave us this green slime to pour in the gaps in the costume, so when he hit that windshield, it splattered for real. It looked just like a bug hitting a windshield! It was absolutely hysterical, and we played it over and over again."

Sometimes the violence of the action sequences proved a little *too* realistic for the final PG cut – including a moment when one of Sarris's guards, played by amputee stuntman Casey Pieretti, has his leg ripped off as he's launched into the air. "It looked horrific," says Armstrong. "It was very funny but too violent for the movie."

CALL TO ACTION

During the action-heavy final act of *Galaxy Quest*, much of Sarris's crew, along with many background Thermians, was made up of stunt performers. "I dialed up the action and tried to include lots of big hits, big collisions, big violence, big things crashing down," Armstrong says. "There was a sequence in which two of Sarris's guys ran into each other so hard that they ended up smashing through the side of the set. One of them came out the other side and knocked himself unconscious! Then when things were blowing up on [Sarris's] ship at the end, we had real fire and a set that really broke apart. The performers were pretty well protected in those suits, but the fire looked big and scary."

A contingent of stunt performers was also integrated into the crowd during the final sequence in which the *Protector*'s command module smashes into the convention center. "I brought in these two performers – one was a huge, muscly guy called Nils Allen Stewart, who was six-foot-four, and the other was Ronald Drown, who was about five-foot-one," Armstrong recalls with a chuckle. "They both had bald heads with little ponytails and we dressed them in identical costumes. Then they get bowled over by all the furniture flying everywhere, along with all these other strange characters. It's very funny if you freeze-frame it!"

DOUBLE TROUBLE

There were stunt doubles for all of the core cast, Armstrong says, including Dennis Fitzgerald (who doubled for Robin Sachs) and John Casino (who doubled for Tim Allen). "Tim had never done action movies before, or even done things like throw a punch on-screen, though he did do several shots featuring real fire towards the end. But a lot of what you think is Tim is actually John. John really studied Tim and dropped some weight to be the same size as him. I'm really proud that we managed to turn Tim Allen into an unlikely but very believable action hero!"

While most of the actors were happy to let their doubles take over for the stunt sequences, one member of the cast wanted to attempt

the action scenes himself – with mixed results. "During the scene in which Alexander Dane charges down the corridor towards the end, smashing into the bad guys, Alan Rickman wanted to do it himself rather than using his double. I remember him saying he wanted to be a 'force of nature!' So we shot the sequence with him – but it didn't look very threatening at all. So when the main unit broke for lunch, I sneakily reshot the footage with his stunt double, Leon Delaney. I don't think Alan ever realized that it wasn't him in that sequence!"

The fact that it's near-on impossible to tell the real actors apart from stunt doubles on-screen is a sign of great stunt work, Armstrong argues. "Stunt work is a craft that should be carefully hidden. It shouldn't be about the ego of the performer doing the action or showing off stunt skills. It should be about making the action right for the story and right for the character. If I looked at *Galaxy Quest* now, I don't think I'd always be able to tell the actors and stunt people apart myself!" ✦

THE FLYING THERMIAN

Galaxy Quest remains a highlight in Armstrong's 50-year career of stunt work. "It was a very, very special movie to do alongside some tremendous people," he enthuses. But the movie has also lodged in his mind for another reason: it is the first movie he worked on with his now-wife, stunt performer Jen Caputo, who played one of the Thermians. However, their first day together on set was not particularly auspicious. "We were testing out a new piece of equipment, an air-ram that throws you up in the air when you step on it. It was supposed to be turned off… but when Jen stood on it, it threw her in the air and span her over. She hit the corner of a lever as she came down and it split her eye open. There was blood everywhere. I sent her to the studio medic, then she went to hospital and had some stitches in her eye. I said, 'You ought to go home now' – but she said she'd rather work! So [makeup head] Ve Neill made her a patch to cover the stitches and she played a Thermian that very day."

Alan Rickman and Tim Allen share a joke on the TV show's alien planet set.

THE TV SHOW

Galaxy Quest's designers and effects artists reveal how they convincingly
staged the late-1970s TV show that had such an impact on Thermian culture.

THE HISTORY OF THE *GALAXY QUEST* TV show that turned Jason Nesmith, Gwen DeMarco, Alexander Dane, Fred Kwan, and Tommy Webber into cult stars is chronicled in the amusing mockumentary *Galaxy Quest 20th Anniversary: The Journey Continues*, made for the E! Television cable network to promote the movie in 1999.

The mockumentary reveals that the show, which ran from 1979 to 1982, was the brainchild of Frank Ross – who originally envisioned it as a Western called *West Quest*. The pilot of *West Quest* had already been shot before "our research people came to us and said that Westerns are out" – at which point the show was quickly rewritten as *Navy Quest*. But with the studio going into bankruptcy and unable to afford to fund a naval drama, the makers of the show took advantage of props left over from "an old space movie they had made" – and so *Galaxy Quest* was born, kicking off with the two-hour pilot, 'The Blue Winds of the Moon.'

The Journey Continues is filled with plenty of other fascinating tidbits about the TV show. In an echo of *Star Trek*, we are told that *Galaxy Quest* initially had trouble finding an audience, but (not

echoing *Star Trek*) became a hit when a World Series game between Pittsburgh and Baltimore was rained out and *Galaxy Quest* was screened in its place.

The mockumentary also fills us in on the background of the show's fictional stars. Jason Nesmith was best known for his role in the "really lame sitcom" *Hello Neighbor*, where "the joke of the show was that you never saw me from the neck down." Jason, we also learn, won the role of Commander Taggart after he accidentally walked into the office of the *Galaxy Quest* casting director, mistaking the audition in progress for an entirely different casting session. "I was halfway through the first season before I realized I wasn't doing *Ordinary People*," Nesmith recalls. No less interesting is the fact that Orson Welles was approached to direct two episodes, including 'The Blibbering Blimp,' a classic installment about a hydrogen-filled alien.

RETRO DESIGNS

The *Galaxy Quest* TV show glimpsed in both the film and mockumentary was brought to life through Linda DeScenna's set design and ILM's model work. DeScenna appears as herself in the

Taggart and his crew on the retro-styled bridge of the *Protector* in the *Galaxy Quest* TV show.

The sets for the TV sequences featured papier-mâché rocks and bare cycloramas.

High School Musical star Corbin Bleu played nine-year-old Tommy.

mockumentary, revealing some of the techniques that were used to create the fictional show. "For other planets we had two types of rocks and we just kept repainting them basically…."

In fact, the style of these TV show sequences was how DeScenna originally envisioned the set design of the entire movie, after conversations with original director Harold Ramis. "Those were the sets we originally built before the concepts [of the rest of the film] changed," she says. "That's how I thought *everything* was going to look: papier-mâché rocks, really cheesy. I had wanted it to look like an old TV show! When we [later] shot those TV show sequences on a stage, there was a real incongruity in my brain. I thought, 'Wait a minute! We can't do this because it doesn't match the new sets!'"

Galaxy Quest's special effects supervisor, Matt Sweeney, also appears in the mockumentary, where he explains the on-set effects that were actually used in the sequence: "It was just kind of a puffing smoke sort of thing, and when the ship would take a disruptor hit, the actors would just dodge left and right and we'd throw things out of the permeance. It was pretty simple." This retro style even extended to the camerawork, with Parisot adding sand to dolly tracks to make the motion less smooth.

For writer Robert Gordon, watching his *Trek*-influenced concepts come to life in these sequences was a dream come true. "It was the most fun day that I was on set for," he says. "To me it was like I got to walk onto the set of *Star Trek* back in the 1960s. They got all of the sets exactly right. There were the bare blue and red cycloramas, and Alan Rickman as Alexander, saying 'By Grabthar's hammer' on these fake plaster of Paris rocks. The sorts of things that were burned into my mind from watching *Trek* when I was growing up."

For two shots in the TV show sequences, a three-foot *Protector* model was utilized that was much less detailed than the eight-foot model used for the rest of the movie. "We really skimped on it – we just painted it white with added decals," laughs model-maker Fon Davis. "But the first time we shot it, it still looked too good! We had to go away and make it look worse."

ILM's visual effects producer Kim Bromley also remembers it being surprisingly difficult to create convincingly low-quality models. "It's hard to make something look bad when your expertise is in making something look great," she points out. "There was more struggle there than you might imagine. It's like when singers with beautiful voices have to pretend to sing poorly. But when we saw the dailies each day, it was such fun. It looked so bad it was great!"

To enhance the retro look of the model sequences, the three-foot

Protector was shot with flat lighting (leading to an even spread of light across the miniature), while compositing supervisor Marshall Krasser also retained matte lines and added scratches to the footage.

However, bearing in mind that the *Galaxy Quest* TV show is supposed to have been filmed in the late '70s/early '80s rather than the original *Star Trek* period of the late '60s, the VFX team needed to be careful not to make things look overly retro. The model sequences of shows of that era such as *Battlestar Galactica* and *Buck Rogers in the 25th Century* proved useful reference points – and as ILM's VFX supervisor Bill George points out, the effects of early 1980s prime-time science fiction were not *that* primitive. "By the time *Battlestar Galactica* had come out, they were using blue-screen photography and motion control. It wasn't that crude. But at the same time, the idea was the show is supposed to be retro in terms of the acting and set design and visual effects and hairstyles. When we first presented the shots of the smaller *Protector* to Dean, we made it look like the ship was being held up with wires. He said, 'No, you've gone too far!'"

The opening sequences for a 1990s sequel series – also called *Galaxy Quest: The Journey Continues* – is seen at the end of the movie, featuring updated, though still far from cutting-edge, sets and visual effects. ✦

Dr. Lazarus ponders the universe amid Stonehenge-like alien monoliths. Top: TV show alien ray gun by Warren Manser.

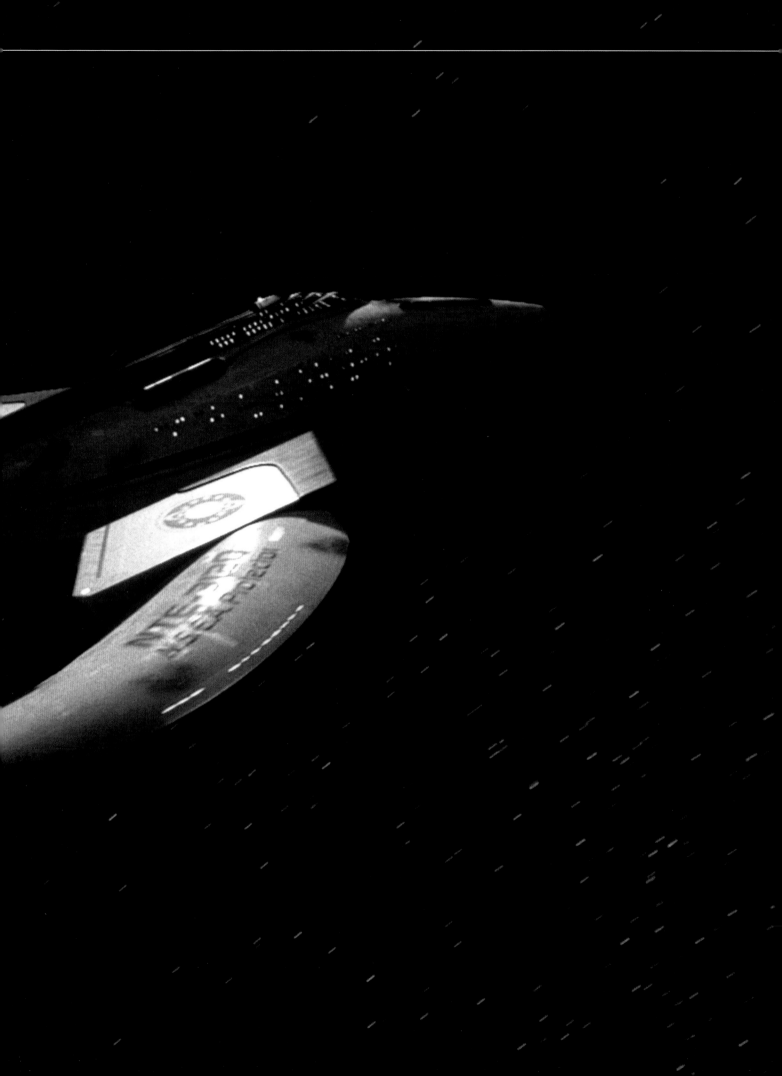

N.S.E.A. PROTECTOR

The design of the heroes' starship was the result of hundreds of concept drawings
and pioneering techniques in both physical and CG model-making.

The *Protector* moves through the spaceport on its maiden voyage. Tiny CG cephalopod worker bees can also be seen in shot.

THE *PROTECTOR* COULDN'T LOOK like the *U.S.S. Enterprise*, that much was clear. Six years before Paramount bought DreamWorks, the latter studio were nervous they'd be sued if *Galaxy Quest*'s starship resembled the iconic *Star Trek* design. "It's the first time I've ever worked on a design where we had to have the legal department involved," laughs ILM's visual effects supervisor, Bill George.

Yet for the story to act as any kind of homage to *Star Trek*, the *Protector* needed to look... well, like the *Enterprise*. "The fear was that we'd have some kind of weird-looking, out-of-time spaceship that didn't honor the concept of a *Star Trek* parody," says visual concept designer Erich Rigling. "It had to feel like the original *Star Trek*."

Getting the balance of *Enterprise*/not-the-*Enterprise* right was quite a conundrum – and it was one that needed to be settled before production designer Linda DeScenna could begin

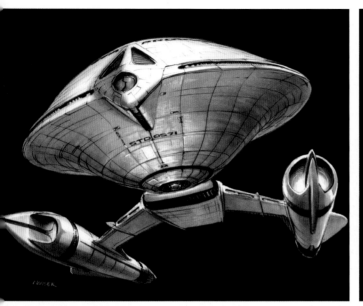

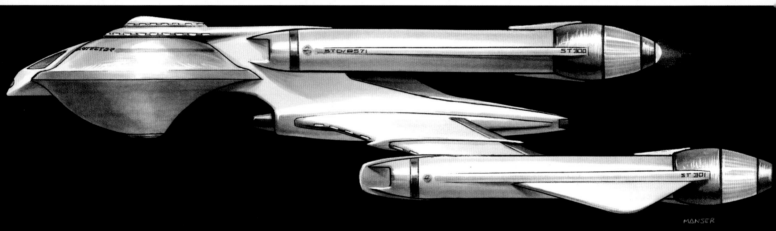

Top left and bottom: Two early *Protector* concept illustrations by Warren Manser. Top right: Alternative *Protector* design by Erich Rigling.

designing the interiors. ILM's art department, as well as the movie's production illustrators, generated hundreds of designs, experimenting with concepts that largely placed an emphasis on clean, plain design shapes. "Eventually, we boiled it down to the shapes [of the *Enterprise*] – the dish and the nacelles – and we came up with a new hybrid of those," says George.

Once ILM had settled upon this idea, Rigling drew up the final fundamental design. "I flopped [the shapes of the *Enterprise*] so that the wings basically became the saucer part and the tube become the body part," he explains. "The aim was to embellish on the simple shapes seen in the original *Star Trek* so that it felt like a modern movie without going overboard."

In order to nail down the ship's form and proportions, Rigling's design was transformed into a 12-inch maquette over the course

of a single night by model shop supervisor Brian Gernand and concept designer John Goodson. Their gray primer maquette would later make a cameo in Brandon's bedroom as a "fan replica" of the *Protector*.

SUBMARINE IN SPACE

With the maquette approved, the model shop extrapolated it out into a three-foot model that was used in the 1980s TV show sequences. While this included details such as intake engine grilles, windows, and basic decals, the design remained deliberately spartan. From here, the model shop extended the design again, this time into the main eight-foot version built by the Thermians in the story. This miniature would require much more detailed decals, textures, and paints than the previous iterations.

THE CG PROTECTOR

In addition to the eight-foot model *Protector*, a CG model was built for the sequence in which Tommy steers the ship out of the starport. The CG version was created by ILM's "Rebel Mac" division, so named because they (unlike ILM's other CG departments) used Macs to render ships. But while they had rendered starships for shots in *Star Trek: First Contact*, *Men in Black*, and *The Phantom Menace*, *Galaxy Quest* went one step further by requiring them to create close-ups of the CG *Protector* that had to blend in seamlessly with the model shots.

"We had lessons on how to paint a spaceship from the model shop, who we felt a really strong connection with," recalls Rebel Mac supervisor Stu Maschwitz, who oversaw the work of CG model-maker Colie Wertz and technical director Andrew Hardaway. "Because they were using [computer-controlled] laser-cutters, the model shop had digital files we could use. We could see from their files which parts of the spaceship were shiny and which were matte, and we used those to texture-map our CG ship. But this was a big deal for us: we had to create an extreme close-up of the front of the ship, showing the nose and dish, with the rest of the ship articulating in the background. It also had to interact with

the plate of the [starport] miniature. Nobody was doing this at ILM at the time."

The fact that their shots depicted the maiden voyage of the pristine *Protector* posed additional challenges. "The *Protector* – like the *Enterprise* – is meant to be this clean, beautiful ship representing an aspirational future. You can't weather it too much, or add details like rust and dents, in the tradition of *Star Wars* ships, so you're robbed of a major tool to suggest scale and realism. Instead, the way that you impart scale is with the windows and little lights – anything that your brain will recognize the size of."

As with the physical model, Rebel Mac also suggested scale through imbuing each of the ship's panels with different levels of sheen. "We added shadows, highlights, and reflections of the soft lighting from the dock. At certain angles, all this detail explodes on the surface. Today, with rendering, that just happens, but back then it wasn't easy. But when we showed [the footage] to the company, it felt like a major collective accomplishment. I was really proud of what my team did. It was right up there in the pantheon of ILM's best model work."

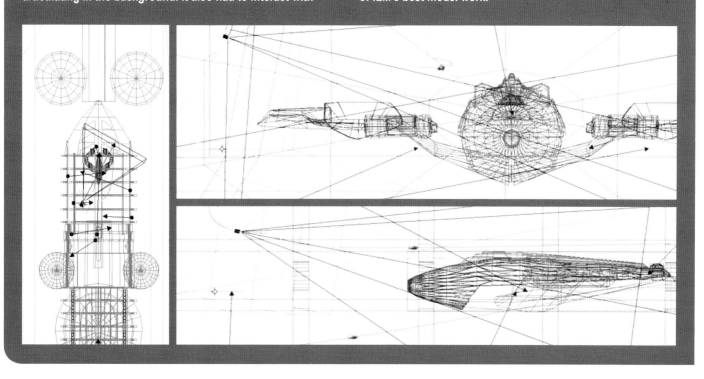

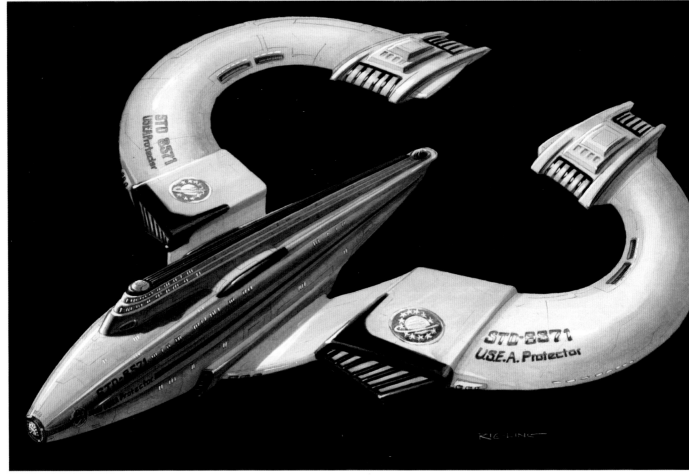

Erich Rigling's final approved design of the *Protector*. The registry STD-8571 can be seen on the wings and hull.

John Goodson was behind many of the design flourishes in the larger model. This included a pattern of *Star Trek*-influenced interlocking panels, and other details inspired by research he had conducted while working on the 1990 thriller, *The Hunt for Red October*. "I remember seeing photos of a *Los Angeles*-class attack submarine that had these interesting bulges on the bow ahead of the conning tower," he says. "It was an interesting detail that I incorporated onto the nose of the *Protector*. I also added what looked like four torpedo doors – something you might find on a World War II submarine – either side of the nose. They opened inwards so a torpedo could be fired."

PERFECTING THE WINGS

While the *Protector*'s hull was sculpted out of urethane foam, many pieces of the ship, from the panels to the deflector dish and the wings, were fabricated using a computer-controlled mill – making it one of the first movies to use this technology. The mill was crucial in ensuring that the two wings of the *Protector*

were perfectly symmetrical. "In model-making, wings are one of the most difficult things you can make – and the wings on the *Protector* were *huge*," says Fon Davis, one of the model-makers who worked on the ship. "They were also wafer-thin and cantilevered out away from the body. At the same time, the wings had to be in perfect alignment or the two engines in the back wouldn't line up properly. It would have been really difficult to make those by hand. So Bryan Dewe, who ran the CNC [computer numerical control] mill, and his team made patterns for the left and right wings, which were then detailed, molded, and cast. They were perfect!" The wings were fitted to a strong but adjustable aluminum structure that allowed the model shop to change their angle while withstanding the cantilevered weight.

The *Protector*'s windows were another key part of the vessel that the model shop needed to get right, as they were critical in imparting a sense of scale to the ship. The shape of the *Protector* made this trickier than creating windows for a starship like the *Enterprise*. "We had to make each window smaller and smaller as it went around the two curved lines," explains Davis. "They had to look perfect, because if the pattern was just a little off it wouldn't look real." The sense of scale given by the windows was further enhanced through illumination provided by a multitude of neon lights.

As well as the *Protector*'s shapes and paneling, the ship's paint scheme also took inspiration from *Star Trek* – for practical reasons as much as anything. "As they did on the *Enterprise*, we painted the whole ship white and broke out different colors on the panels – the light grays, the different shades of white," Davis explains. "The other *Star Trek* aesthetic we used was painting the panels with slightly metallic, opalescent 'interference colors,' which is something used on certain cars. It's a clear coat with a powder in it that changes color depending on what angle you view it. We painted on interference gold, interference blue, interference purple and red... all these different colors. Because the shape of the ship is a compound curve, all these tiny little panels would appear and

disappear in different colors as you went around it. This complex array of panels was a subtle but creative way of selling the scale of the ship."

Once the paints had been applied, the model shop added decals, including registries and a patchwork of shapes. These were largely designed by Goodson, who, as model-maker on *Star Trek VI* and model supervisor on *Generations* and *First Contact*, knew which *Trek* tricks could be effectively transported onto the *Protector*. "I remember in the original series of *Star Trek*, the *Enterprise* had these patterns along the belly of the ship," Goodson says. "I had already put those markings on the bottom of the ship in *First Contact* as a homage, and I mimicked it again with the *Protector*. You can see those details when the ship flips after going through the minefield, though it's very subtle. We also used Letraset dry transfers to add the lettering and numbers on the model, as well as little dots and dashes."

ILM's model shop at work on the Protector. Left to right: John Duncan, Brian Gernand, Fon Davis, Kim Smith (underneath), John Goodson, and Grant Imahara.

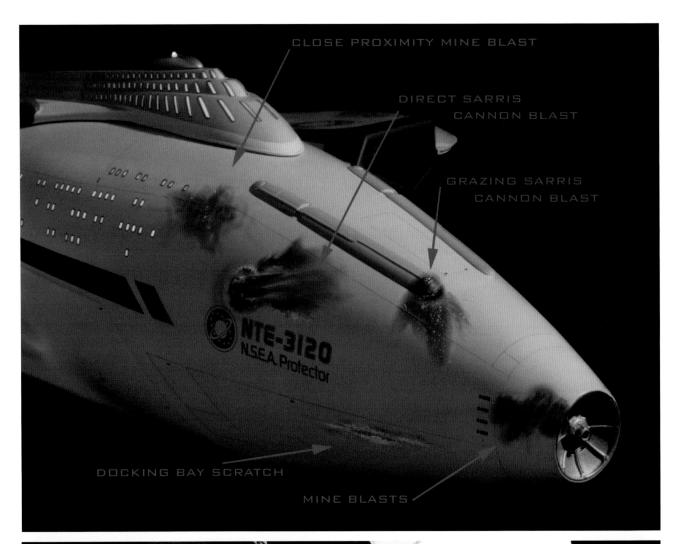

CLOSE PROXIMITY MINE BLAST

DIRECT SARRIS
CANNON BLAST

GRAZING SARRIS
CANNON BLAST

NTE-3120
N.S.E.A. Protector

DOCKING BAY SCRATCH

MINE BLASTS

Top: ILM artwork displaying areas of the ship damaged by mines and cannons. Bottom: The eight-foot model is filmed on the motion control stage.

The bright blue glow of the ship's engines was created with a special lenticular material and computer-controlled LEDs.

Elsewhere, the blue glow of the forward and rear engines was made using a lenticular material that Goodson had spotted on a bookmark at a nature-themed gift company, which was then backlit using computer-controlled LEDs. "It was this almost holographic material that had a repeated dot pattern in it," he remembers. "I was really taken with it, so we tracked down what it was!"

SMALL WORLD

Besides these exterior details, the model shop constructed entire miniature rooms for those moments when viewers could see beyond the ship's windows. "The rooms had tiny slides in each window and a very complex lighting system to illuminate them," remembers Davis.

Once the model was fully built and approved, it was shot against blue screen on ILM's motion control stage over six months, a process overseen by co-visual effects supervisor Ed Hirsh – another veteran of ILM's *Star Trek* projects. The vast collective *Trek* experience of so many of the VFX team, combined with the new techniques and original flourishes that they brought to the movie, ensured that the final ship successfully met the brief: here was a vessel that could fit into the *Star Trek* universe without resembling the *Enterprise* too slavishly. A lawsuit was avoided.

Today, the eight-foot *Protector* model hangs in a stairwell at ILM's headquarters in San Francisco. ✦

WHAT'S IN A NAME?

The *Protector*'s lawsuit-fearing history is amusingly referenced in its NTE-3120 registry: "NTE" being an acronym for "Not the Enterprise," something coined by VFX production assistant Sam Stewart. Up until this point the ship had gone by the more risqué registry of "STD-8571" (visible in the decals of the maquette, above right), a legacy from the slightly broader tone the movie had during early preproduction. The ship was also originally called the "*U.S.E.A. Protector*" rather than N.S.E.A. This was a name that had been innocently devised by writer Robert Gordon until someone pointed out its potential double meaning.

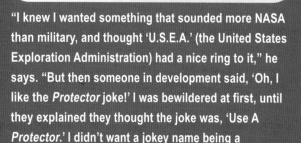

"I knew I wanted something that sounded more NASA than military, and thought 'U.S.E.A.' (the United States Exploration Administration) had a nice ring to it," he says. "But then someone in development said, 'Oh, I like the *Protector* joke!' I was bewildered at first, until they explained they thought the joke was, 'Use A *Protector*.' I didn't want a jokey name being a distraction, so I changed it to N.S.E.A."

INSIDE THE PROTECTOR

The *Protector*'s maze of high-tech rooms and corridors was designed and constructed by the production's art, props, and visual effects departments...

THE BRIDGE

Like *Star Trek*, much of the action in *Galaxy Quest* takes place on the *Protector*'s bridge, so it was a crucial set to get right. But, as with the design of the ship's exterior, DreamWorks was fearful of being sued by Paramount if the bridge looked *too* familiar. In fact, the original bridge design by Linda DeScenna's art department – generated when Harold Ramis was directing and the movie had a more 1960s-style aesthetic – did more closely resemble that of the *Enterprise*. However, when Dean Parisot took over, there was a drive to imbue the set with a more modern sheen, and artists,

including Alex McDowell and Simon Murton, worked up new concepts for the location.

The final bridge design retained a flavor of the *Enterprise* layout – the captain's chair, positions for the navigator, comms officer, and executive officer – but it also reflected the layout of a nautical bridge that had influenced *Star Trek* in the first place. The bridge was also given a sleek, futuristic feel worthy of the Thermians' engineering talents. Though there are a few hints at the alien science beyond the surface gloss, such as the blue glow emanating from Tommy's joystick (and elsewhere, a blue-splattered wall behind Mathesar

Bridge concept illustration by Simon Murton.

as he enters the strategy room), Parisot was originally intending to make this more explicit. "We shot a number of sequences where a panel would fall off the wall and you would see this blue liquid going through tubes," says ILM's VFX supervisor, Bill George. "Dean wanted to get across the fact that, even though what you're seeing was based on an old TV show, there was this fantastic advanced technology behind it."

The movie's special and visual effects teams deployed some advanced technology, too. In contrast to the footage of the old *Galaxy Quest* TV show – where an attack on the bridge was created

through camera wobbles and the actors throwing themselves from side to side – the main bridge set was constructed on a large gimbal that hurled the cast around for real during battle sequences.

Meanwhile, the captain's chair was so advanced that the upholstery never crumpled when Jason sat in it – a result of VFX house Light Matters digitally removing wrinkles in post. "That chair prop weighed about 150 pounds, as it had all of this electronic stuff in," adds stage foreman John Rutchland, who oversaw its installation. "But like on *Star Trek*, the chair was a big deal. The prop house did a great job. It was really a work of art."

CREW QUARTERS

While the Thermians reside in spartan dormitories, the command crew are given their own quarters. Rooms include Gwen's glamorous boudoir ("They designed it based on the Tauren Pleasure Ship from historical document 37!" Gwen exclaims in one of Robert Gordon's early drafts), and Alexander's quarters, which consists of a bed of spikes and a toilet-from-hell.

Like other rooms on the ship, the quarters were largely the result of Linda DeScenna's overall vision and concepts from her art team, who included Warren Manser, Wil Rees, and Guy Hendrix Dyas. DeScenna remembers that the crew quarters were some of the sets to undergo significant changes once the design of the movie shifted away from a low-budget, 1960s-style aesthetic. "Gwen's boudoir was originally much cheesier, much less designed, so we changed that quite a lot," she says. "But then we didn't see her quarters at all [in the final film]!" Alexander's "bedroom," like Gwen's quarters, was also cut from the final edit.

MESS HALL

The *Protector*'s freshly arrived command crew get to enjoy their first meal in the mess hall. Mathesar explains that their meals have been generated by the Thermians' "food synthesizer" based on the regional menu of their birthplace – which means corn-fed Iowa beef steak for Jason (a homage to Captain Kirk's place of birth), French cuisine for Gwen (specified in an early draft), spaghetti for Guy, and Kep-mop blood ticks for Alexander ("Just like Mother used to make"). It's all washed down with a strange blue liquid that echoes the substance found inside the walls of the ship.

The design of the mess hall drew on the smooth curves of the ship's exterior, including a quadrant-shaped dining table and a ceiling of concentric circles. "Linda had a clean, straightforward design aesthetic in mind for the *Protector*, and we had to capture the essence of the designs without unnecessary clutter," remembers production illustrator Warren Manser.

STRATEGY ROOM

The strategy room, seen when the command crew gather to assess the damage from the Tothian mines, is the movie's take on *Star Trek*'s briefing rooms. The diagnostics on the room's viewscreens were added in postproduction by Light Matters (as were viewscreen shots on the bridge). "That display was another non-blue-screen composite," remembers Light Matters' supervisor

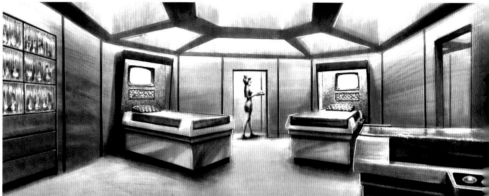

Mat Beck. "We had to insert graphics behind foreground actors, along with table reflections, and track to the environment as the camera moved around."

SHUTTLE BAY

The shuttle bay area, filled with Thermian personnel, multiple shuttlecraft, rigs, and cranes, was a composite of assorted elements. "They built one shuttle and a piece of floor on stage, which they shot against blue screen with the actors," explains VFX art director Alex Jaeger. "I did a design of a vast, multilevel shuttlebay showing that the platform they're on is actually above a much wider area. It was an attempt to make the ship feel much bigger than a ship you'd find on *Star Trek*." The live-action footage was composited in with digital matte paintings by Yusei Uesugi based on Jaeger's concepts, along with green-screen footage of the Thermian technical crew.

GENERATOR ROOM

The kind of place where Scotty or La Forge work up a sweat, the generator room contains the quantum flux drive, which is overseen by Fred Kwan and his more knowledgeable Thermians. At the heart of the drive is the beryllium sphere, which resembles *The Next*

Generation's dilithium reactor. In early drafts of Robert Gordon's script, the beryllium sphere was a "carbonite sphere."

DIGITAL CONVEYOR ROOM

Robert Gordon knew he needed to have an equivalent of *Star Trek*'s transporter room – he just wasn't sure of a convincing alternative moniker to "transporter." "I had all these names like the 'atom freeway' – it was really hard," Gordon remembers. "And I didn't want it to sound *too* much like *Star Trek*." He settled on "molecular conveyor" in his early drafts, before this was changed to "digital conveyor."

OTHER AREAS

Another classic *Star Trek* location is the medical bay. Though Warren Manser drew up detailed concept art of the facility (pictured above), it is only glimpsed in the background for a matter of seconds during Mathesar's initial tour of the ship ("The organ fabrication chamber is coming along nicely," he informs the crew.) Other rooms seen briefly in the movie include the "media room" (where Tommy watches historical documents to learn how to fly the ship) and the reactor core unit. In Gordon's early drafts, the latter (along with the Chompers) was located within a "manufacturing cavern" – an automated facility for ship maintenance described as resembling Dante's Inferno.

SURFACE POD

The small shuttlecraft used by the *Galaxy Quest* cast to travel to the mining planet was styled on the approved design of its mother ship.

The underside of the surface pod, as seen in this CG footage of the vessel landing on the mining planet, reveals its registry is 2.

THE SHUTTLECRAFT IS AN INTEGRAL part of the *Star Trek* universe, from the *Galileo* in the Original Series episode 'The Galileo Seven' to the Type-15 shuttle in *The Next Generation* and the Travel Pod in *The Motion Picture*. *Galaxy Quest* introduced its own take on the concept, in the form of the surface pod that the heroes use to travel to the Crystal Planet (as the desert world was originally named).

While other ships were largely brought to life with miniatures, a full-size surface pod was constructed for the movie. This was shot against blue screen for the sequence in the shuttlebay and then crated to Goblin Valley for the scenes on the planet. "The design was fairly simple, as we had to keep in mind they needed to build it practically," says visual effects supervisor Bill George. "The full-size version was pretty cool, but if you look inside there is absolutely no detailing. That was another reflection of something you'd seen in *Star Trek*."

By the time ILM began designing the shuttle, the *Protector* design had been approved, and the shuttle needed to fit in with the look of the larger ship. "We wanted to honor the geometry and the style of the *Protector*," says the film's concept designer, Erich Rigling. "I originally had the ramp coming down from the nose so that you walked down from between the two pilot seats. It looked a little bit wider and sleeker. The final design didn't change that much, but they [the production art department] made it a little deeper and more shaped like the proportions of the *Galileo*."

ILM also created a CG shuttle for shots of the ship flying, taking off, and landing, using computer graphics tools they had honed while working on *Star Trek Generations*. The point-of-view shot of the shuttle flying was achieved through speeded-up helicopter footage overseen by second unit director and creative advisor Stefen Fangmeier. ✦

Top: A full-size ship was built for static exterior and interior shots of the surface pod. Above: A CG version, based on the full-size model, was used for shots of the shuttle taking off.

COMMAND MODULE

The command module's dramatic crash into the convention center
was one of ILM's biggest effects sequences on *Galaxy Quest*.

JUST AS THE STARSHIP *ENTERPRISE*-D occasionally disengages its saucer section during emergencies, the *Protector*'s nose (or "command module") is able to break away from the hull to operate as a separate vessel as needed.

Shots of the command module separating from the *Protector* and hurtling toward Earth were accomplished with a six-foot miniature, while a full-size prop was built for the final sequence in which the dazed actors emerge from the module at the fan convention. A third, one-sixth-scale module was constructed for the miniature crash – one of ILM's biggest set pieces on the movie.

Built from steel tubing and sheet metal, the one-sixth-scale command module was, in fact, merely the nose section – a mandrel lacking almost all the detailing of the six-foot model. "It was [digitally] replaced [in post], so its job was just to blast its way through," explains Michael Lynch, lead model-maker on the ship and miniature convention center. "It had the correct geometry and a texture paint job, as all the debris needed to break and shed off that shape, but it was kind of a blunt instrument."

Before the crash could be engineered, an entire swathe of the convention center needed to be built in miniature. Chief model-maker Barbara Affonso oversaw the construction of hundreds of

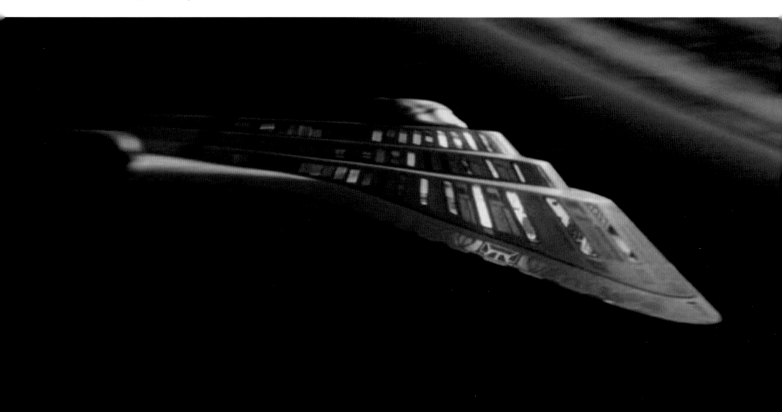

A six-foot miniature was built by ILM's model shop for the sequence in which the module breaks away and heads toward the convention center.

Dave Lowery's storyboards and stills from the film show how the command module separates from the *Protector*.

pieces of miniature memorabilia, which included everything from *Galaxy Quest* banners to tiny VHS tapes of effects-heavy movies such as *The Last Starfighter* and *Daylight*. Meanwhile, Lynch painstakingly measured and photographed the dressed Hollywood Palladium set to ensure his recreation matched the real location as closely as possible.

The miniature stage, tables, and memorabilia were all constructed from scored, three-quarter-inch sheets of Pyrocil – a type of plaster with citric acid and sodium bicarbonate – which would break apart easily on impact. But as Lynch explains, it wasn't the easiest material to work with. "It was as though you put an Alka-Seltzer in plaster; it fizzed up and created bubbles. That made it very lightweight – and, consequently, very weak, allowing it to break up into pieces. But you had to take great pains to handle the material carefully as it was so fragile. It was like building a house of cards. Once you got toward the end, it just took one false move or somebody not paying attention for it all to fall down. It got a little tense!"

The module composited in with footage shot at Santa Anita racetrack; the partly rotoscoped crash sequence; Sarris emerges, with added digital effects by ILM.

CRASH AND BURN

Once the miniatures were completed, Brian Gernand's model shop crew glued down anything that they didn't want to shoot through the air during the crash. Weighted fishing lines were attached to other sections to make them fly in desired directions.

The command module mandrel was fixed to a track beneath the elevated stage and connected to a hydraulic ram that would propel it into the miniature convention center. To make the crash appear even more devastating, practical effects supervisor Geoff Heron rigged a series of pyrotechnics that would trigger as the command module shot forward.

Bearing in mind that there were only enough miniatures for two full crashes (plus insert shots), there was little scope for anything to go wrong. At the same time, they had to follow rigorous safety precautions in case anything *did* go wrong. "That ship had to go from zero to about 20 miles per hour to a complete stop, all within a small stage space," recalls David Dranitzke, stage manager of the sequence (along with many of ILM's other miniature crashes). "There was a lot of planning and preparation. You want things to break apart the way you need them to for camera. You don't want a miniature folding table flying up, smacking the lens and covering up the crash! Geoff Heron and his crew were extremely cautious, making sure that all the bolts were in place and that the path of the ship was completely clear so that if anything went wrong, it would just smash into the stage door."

Finally, came the moment everyone was waiting for. The model-makers who had spent weeks painstakingly building the miniatures, including Lynch and Affonso, gathered at a safe distance to watch their beautiful work be blown apart. "It was pretty loud and destructive," says Dranitzke. "The whole thing was over in a couple seconds, though it's four to five times longer with the cuts in the movie. We had a crack team who were at the top of their game, so everything went to plan."

The miniature crash was composited in with shots of stunt performers at the real convention center, and enhanced with both digitally simulated debris and real dust elements generated by mortar cannons. Happily, not all of the models were destroyed in the explosion. "I still have sections of the miniature convention floor," says Dranitzke. "I use them for sushi trays." ✦

LIGHTS, CAMERA, ACTION!

To make it look as if the full-size module was crashing through the wall, the sequence was shot at 72 frames per second and enhanced with particle smoke. "I chose a very low camera angle, which required cutting out a section of the set floor to accommodate a small high-speed camera," remembers miniature director of photography Pat Turner (pictured right). "The lighting was a challenge as I needed a lot of depth of field to keep everything in focus and duplicate the real convention center. We also had to [duplicate] the sunlight blasting through the set after the crash." To meet these needs, Turner used a large 18K HMI light that bounced off a mirror, as well as an array of smaller lights. One side effect of this, though, was it made the set extraordinarily hot. "It was pretty hard on the miniature," Turner says. "We could only have the lights on for a short time otherwise we'd melt the set!"

THERMIAN DOCKING STRUCTURE #6
DYAS 99 'GALAXY QUEST'

One of Guy Hendrix Dyas's early concepts for the Thermian starport, created with gouache and colored pencils.

STARPORT

The riblike interior of the Thermians' docking station was based on a manta ray's throat – but building the model without the whole thing collapsing was an engineering challenge.

IKE SHUTTLES, SPACE STATIONS, and starships, spacedocks are an essential part of *Star Trek* history. *Galaxy Quest* has its own take on the spacedock, a starport situated above the remains of the alien species' decimated homeworld, Thermia.

Concept illustrator Guy Hendrix Dyas – later production designer on movies such as *Inception* and *Passengers* – worked up a series of concepts for the exterior of the docking station. Though never seen on-screen, it provided useful reference for ILM when it came to visualizing the structure's interior. "The design had to take itself

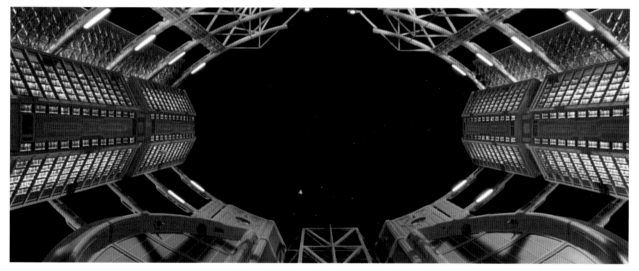

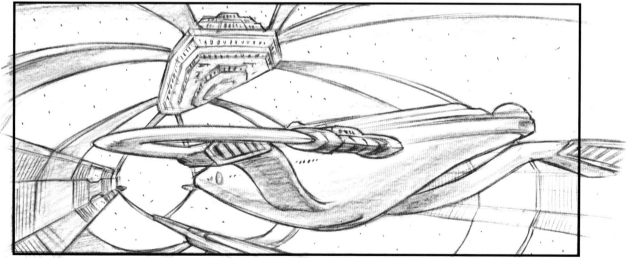

The starport model as seen in the film, and Kirk Henderson's storyboard showing the *Protector*'s passage through the dock.

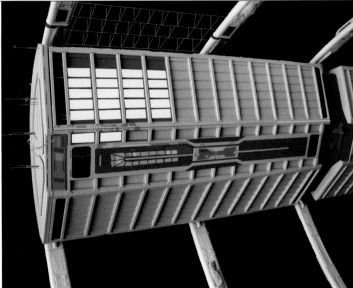

Kirk Henderson's effects storyboard showing the Thermians looking out as the ship passes; CAD model of the spaceport used to plan out color details.

seriously – it would have fallen apart if it had been too jokey," Dyas says. "We [production illustrators] took a sort of natural aesthetic from the look of *Star Trek* and *Deep Space Nine* for designs like this: shiny surfaces, molded soft corners, and stark colors with pastel shades."

Designing the interior of the starport involved working up dozens of evolving iterations, according to ILM's visual effects art director Alex Jaeger. "It went from something that felt more organic to something we could realistically build," he says. "We also had to make sure we knew the color scheme of the space station and that it tied into everything else. We came up with a purplish-blue tone – the model

itself was very purple, but it was a little grainier blue on film."

The final look of the starport was created by concept designer John Goodson. "We knew what the exit looked like because of Guy Dyas's drawing but had no idea of what the interior looked like," he recalls. "But then I came across a picture looking down a manta ray's throat. It had this interesting gill pattern there – and you can see that pattern behind the *Protector* [as it flies out of the docking station]. I did a fleshed out drawing that was about 11 inches tall and three feet wide, taping pieces of paper together so you could see both ends of the thing."

The model starport and *Protector* were shot separately on motion control stages and composited together. A CG *Protector* was also used in part of the scene.

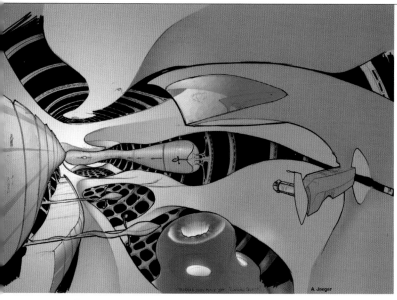

Alex Jaeger's concept art of the structure, complete with Thermians looking out; visual effects supervisor Bill George inspects the full-size model.

EVERYTHING IS ILLUMINATED

Don Bies was the lead model-maker of the 17-foot starport miniature. As a starting point, Bies used a CAD program to create a 3D version of Goodson's sketch. From there, he and his team laser-cut the pieces of the model and assembled them into the structure – but the skeletal design did pose some difficulties. "It was a unique challenge in that it's a very spindly model," he says. "We had to be able to remove sections on one side so they could shoot the model without the other side falling apart. It had to look fragile yet still be rigid enough to hold together. That took quite a bit of engineering."

To ensure that the model wouldn't simply collapse, it was suspended on – and held together by – a steel frame. The structure itself consisted of two joined sections. The first was the back section – essentially a set of vacuum-formed, repeating rib shapes lit by a fluorescent tube. The second section was the front viewing gallery where the Thermians watch the *Protector* depart. "They filmed the line-up of actors playing the Thermians in L.A., and then we took the actual film strips and popped them inside the model," says Bies.

The transparent film slides helped to give the watching Thermians a feeling of depth, adds Fon Davis, another of the starport's model-makers. "We illuminated the line-up of Thermians with four off-the-shelf light bulbs. The problem was it could easily have looked like a light box and give away the fact it was a miniature. So what we did was take colored gels – one was slightly yellow, one slightly green, one slightly orange – and put those gels in front of the slides in random order throughout the windows. It meant that the color temperature of each window varied. That's something they do in high-rise buildings. So even though each window is only about an inch-and-a quarter wide and half-an-inch tall, it looks big, and we sold the scale of the windows."

In addition to the 17-foot model used in the majority of the scene, a separate four-foot front piece was built by Adam Savage for the moment in which the *Protector* scrapes along the side of the starport. Though it is one of the funniest sequences in the film, at the time Jaeger wasn't sure they would pull it off convincingly. "Getting the nose to scrape on the edge of the docking ring isn't actually possible because of the way the wings and nacelles extend out!" he laughs. "The nose can't physically go up against the wall. But as we did it in two passes – and you don't actually see how the wing interacts – you don't really notice." ✦

Model-makers Nelson Hall and Danny Wagner at work on the front section of Sarris's ship in ILM's model shop.

THE FALCON

ILM's model shop recall building a sinister ship that featured
UV paint, teethlike spikes – and resembled a "mummified dead fish"…

SARRIS'S WARSHIP IS AN ORGANIC vessel that boasts extensive weapons and shields, including implosion missiles and neutron armor. Though the ship wasn't named in the movie, it was called the *Falcon* in Robert Gordon's early drafts – a "placeholder name" that had echoes of a Klingon bird-of-prey, according to Gordon. It was later rechristened the *K'ragk Vort't* (translating as the "angry shellfish of doom") in the *Galactopedia* guide, written by *Star Trek Encyclopedia* authors Michael and Denise Okuda for the film's Blu-ray release.

The look of the *Falcon/K'ragk Vort't* reflects the belligerent nature of the Sarris Dominion, and its dank, green interiors and scaly exterior are in stark contrast to the clean, smooth design of the *Protector*. The ship was designed by Linda DeScenna's art department before being built by ILM's model-makers. "We based the ship on Stan Winston's approved concept drawings for the character [Sarris] – the 'Green Monster' as we called him," says DeScenna. "His ship was based on elements of his body. I wanted it to be very spiky and kind of camouflaged."

The front of the *Falcon* was designed to resemble a mouth, echoing the planet killer from the *Star Trek* episode, 'The Doomsday Machine.'

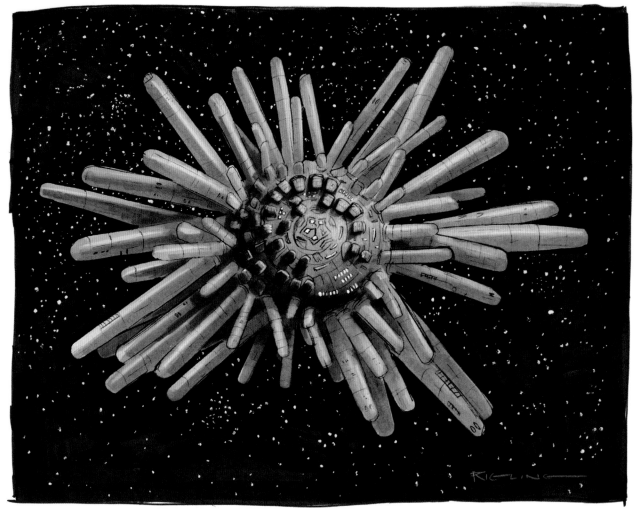

In this very different take on the *Falcon* by ILM concept designer Erich Rigling, the vessel resembles a sea urchin.

"It was designed to give the audience a visual clue that these are the bad guys and their spaceship is nastier, more organic, more alien," adds ILM's VFX supervisor Bill George. "The glow of the ship also gave it a cool effect that was like [*Star Trek* episode] 'The Doomsday Machine.'"

Before the final design had been settled upon, several other interesting concepts for the ship were explored by both the production and ILM art departments. ILM concept designer Erich Rigling remembers some of his earlier iterations. "At one point we did one that [resembled] a World War II sub but with Gothic arches. Then, because Sarris is a sea creaturey guy, I started working with shell motifs and shapes. I found this picture of a sea urchin with really big spikes – almost pencillike things that radiate all around it, some big, some small. I drew something like that and put it in space with lights all around it. Bill [George] was like, 'That's it, man! We gotta do that right there!' At that exact moment, the other [production] art department pitched the final Sarris ship design. So my design didn't make it – it was pretty cool though!"

THE DEAD FISH

ILM's model shop drew up refined illustrations of the design and sculpted a one-foot resin maquette to nail down the broad strokes of the model. Concept designer and model-maker John Goodson used the maquette as a leaping-off point to work up detailed drawings of the bridge, the inside of the mouth, and the ship's missiles. "The ship reminded me of a mummified dead fish!" he laughs.

"The real challenge in the design was trying to make sure that it felt big and had a complexity to it, while also being organic and weird," says lead model-maker Fon Davis. "In [most] spacecraft, you have panels and windows and ladders and doors – things that cue the human brain as to what size something is. But with Sarris's ship there was really none of that. There was a lot of concept work in figuring out the texture."

Once the maquette had been approved, the model shop set to work on constructing the eight-foot, 1/300-scale version. The miniature was assembled from large pieces built by different teams of model-makers and incorporated several unusual techniques. "Most of the time we do 'hard surface' models for spacecraft and softer, sculpted [models] for creatures," says Davis. "But Sarris's ship almost had the aesthetic of a creature. So we ended up sculpting the whole thing out of Roma clay, then making molds and casting it in fiberglass. The exception was the inside of the mouth – that was made using vacuum-formed clear plastic, so we could put lights behind it. [Lead sculptor] Danny Wagner created this slimy, creepy look inside the mouth with incredible airbrushing and veins. It had tons and tons of little teethlike spikes."

Wagner clearly remembers his thought process for sculpting the ship's cavernous mouth. "It was very bony and stretchy, and the clear vac [vacuformed areas around the lights] were like organic windows," he says. "In building the ship it helped us to think of it as an actual character that was alive and had organic parts. It wasn't mentioned in the script, but I imagined that the actual organic saliva of this creature would slide towards the glowing light at the center of the mouth, which actually helps the ship stay alive. This supports the whole system of the ship and its organic parts to make it stay strong and fly fast."

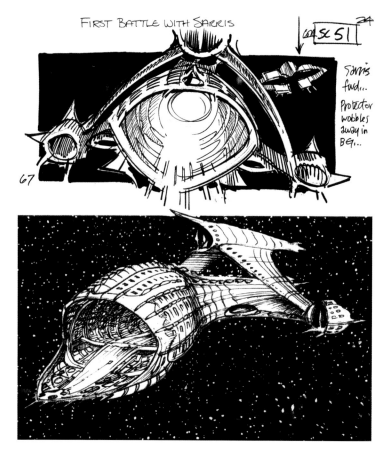

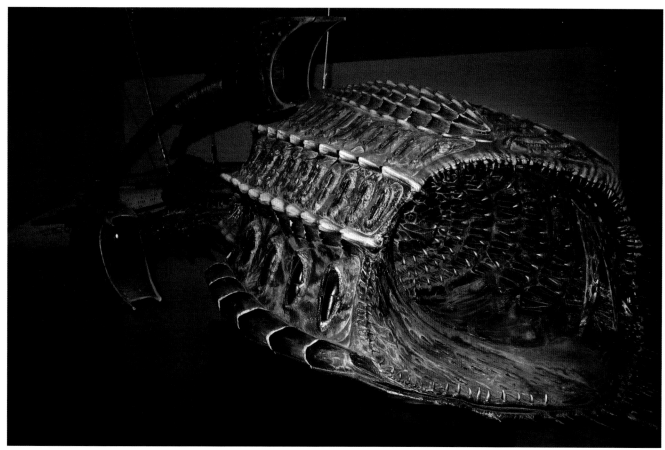

Above: The *Falcon* model hangs in ILM's office alongside the *Protector*. Top: Storyboard panel by Dave Lowery and production illustration by Mike Swift.

Lead sculptor Danny Wagner and lead model-maker Fon Davis assemble the segments of the ship around the motion control rod.

Another striking feature of the ship was the antenna array that protrudes from the lower front section of the ship, something that Davis remembers as being a headache to construct. Because the antennas were so small, the only way the model-makers could build anything strong enough at that size was to solder brass together. "They stuck out so far that when anyone walked by the model, they would inevitably snag a piece of their clothes on them," Davis recalls. "You kept having to repair them!"

All three of the ship's intake engines had lights embedded into them by Davis, model-maker Jon Foreman, and the late electrical engineer and *MythBusters* presenter, Grant Imahara. "There was a very complex electrical system inside the model that was connected to an umbilical which fed electricity into it," says Davis. "Grant designed and programmed the magical pattern of blue light inside the engines using a circuit board. That was all practical rather than CG."

To make it look as if light was seeping out through the scales, the model featured another, even more unusual lighting technique. "I'd read about a technique they had used on an episode of *Star Trek: The Next*

Generation ['Identity Crisis'] in which LeVar Burton gets turned into this blue lizardlike creature," recalls John Goodson. "They did that using this UV light system called Foxfire: they painted him with UV paint, which lit up when these emitters were switched on. It gave Sarris's ship that weird, yellowish glow."

The UV paint was added in virtual darkness by Davis and model shop supervisor Brian Gernand after the ship's standard acrylic brown and green paints had been applied. "We airbrushed in the fluorescent green and yellow gradients under each of the scaly shapes on the body of the ship," Davis says. "When we switched on the blacklights – just before they fire a missile or take off – you could see this super-bright fluorescent color."

At the center of the model was a heavy steel rod that could be connected to various segments of the ship to move it in different directions during filming on the motion control stage. As with the *Protector*, it was shot against blue screen with the starfield backdrop added during the compositing stage. Today, the model proudly hangs at the ILM office in San Francisco along with the miniature *Protector*. ✦

Sarris and his henchmen on the command deck of the *Falcon*. The dank, green look of the ship echoed the design of Sarris himself.

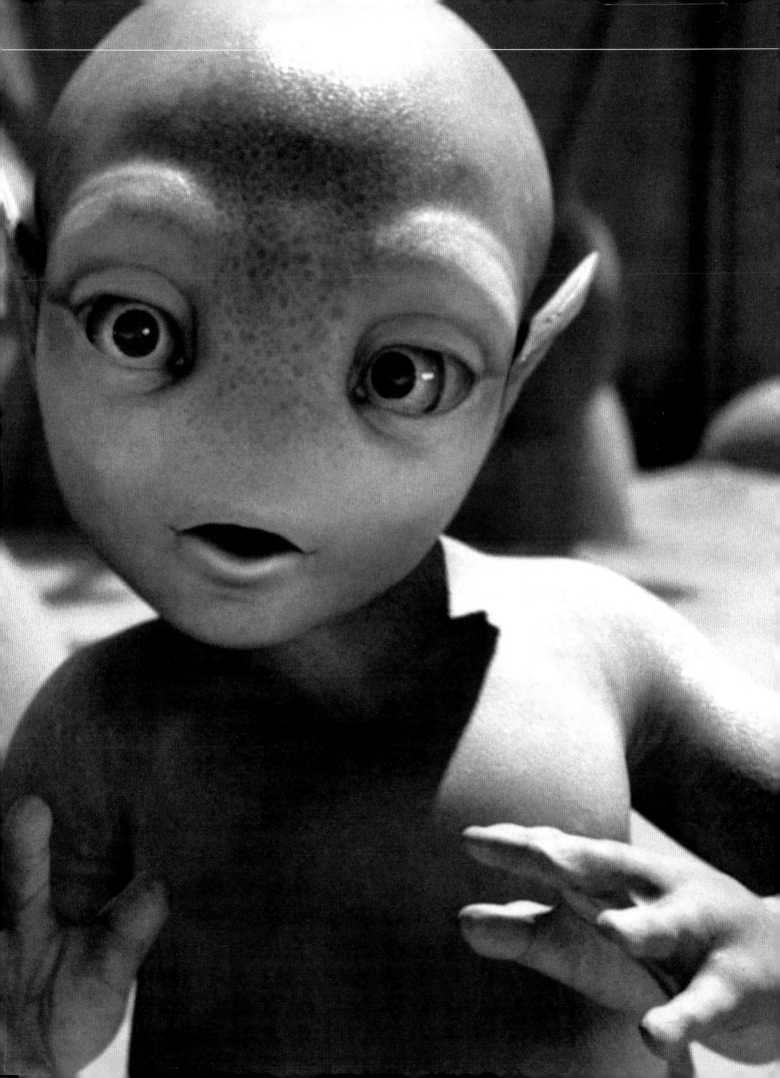

Simon Bisley

One of Simon Bisley's preliminary drawings depicting the Thermians as cute, vulnerable squids.

Copyright © 1999 Stan Winston Studio

THE THERMIANS

The story of how the denizens of Thermia evolved from
sketches of cute squids into full-size mechanical marvels.

IT WAS 3AM AND BRITISH COMIC book artist Simon Bisley needed an animal. He wasn't sure what animal yet, but he was hoping a nature book by everyone's favorite naturalist David Attenborough might help him decide. Bisley had been given the loosest of briefs by Stan Winston: he was to design a sympathetic creature known as a Thermian. The script specified it should have tentacles. Beyond that, he could let his imagination roam free – as long as he came with up something fast. "I had no idea what to do," Bisley recalls. "What was it going to look like? Weirdly, I started to think about *Predator*. Because if you look at it, its face is like a crab's head poking out the top of the shell and its eyes work like a crab too. So I figured, if I can just find a different animal, I can use that."

The early morning nature-reading session paid off. There, on a page of Attenborough's tome, an animal stared out at him. "I thought, wow, a squid, that'll do!" Bisley cackles. "There you go, Stan – there's your creature!"

Although other top artists like Berni Wrightson, Brom, and Jordu

The Thermians arrive to examine the stars of *Galaxy Quest*. The medical devices were clutched by independently puppeteered insert tentacles.

Copyright © 1999 Stan Winston Studio

Above: Christopher Swift sculpts a clay maquette. Right: Crash McCreery's final design.

Copyright © 1999 Stan Winston Studio

Schell also came up with interesting tentacled designs for the Thermians, it was Bisley's vibrant, vulnerable, and wonderfully endearing squids that captured everyone's imagination. The concept was refined by art director Crash McCreery into something that could be practically built and puppeteered, and sculpted into a clay maquette by Christopher Swift in order to work out the fine details. Once the design had been given the final seal of approval, Stan Winston's artists got ready to build some Thermians.

INSIDE THE ALIENS

Five full-size blinking, breathing silicone Thermians were constructed for the movie, each of which boasted 45 tentacles. Around a dozen separate, independently puppeteered 'insert tentacles' were also made that could clutch nightmarish medical devices or whirl around during the Fred/Laliari love scene.

Richard Landon was the animatronics supervisor given the job of figuring out how the mechanics of the Thermians would work. Though Landon and Winston had early discussions about cutting a hole in the stage to hand-puppeteer parts of the creature, the idea was quickly discarded in favor of cable- and pulley-controlled head and body movements and electronically actuated interior motion. To make the faces of the puppets more expressive, the eyelids were electronically linked to the movement of the eyeballs. This feature was enhanced by Landon's idea of having the Thermians' eyes bulge in and out as they warble away during the examination scene.

Landon remembers the biggest challenge in building the Thermians was the tight schedule – especially after it suddenly became tighter. "One of the things that Stan liked to do was to pull the rug out from underneath us a bit in some of our timing," he laughs. "I remember that on the original schedule, we were supposed to show up on set with just the tentacles for the subjective shots of medical devices approaching the cast during the examination scene. This was going to be the first time the cast had ever seen the Thermians, and Stan said to us, 'I know we were supposed to have several more weeks to build the bodies but I want the actors to be able to see the entirety of the Thermians. I want them to be able to get an accurate eyeline and a reaction to how crazy these things look.' So we lost close to a month of the build schedule. But everybody worked long

Clockwise from top left: Shane Mahan and his team sculpt a Thermian; Stan Winston and Richard Landon examine an animatronic head; testing a puppet's electronics.

Copyright © 1999 Stan Winston Studio

Mathesar reverts to his tentacled form while being tortured by Sarris's guards. The sequence was enhanced with CG effects in postproduction.

and hard to make sure that we did what Stan asked us to do."

The team's heroic efforts paid off and the Thermians were completed ahead of time. Yet the curtailed schedule was far from the only shock in store for the studio. Effects supervisor Shane Mahan remembers the moment he got a call informing him of some unwelcome news. "The [Thermian] characters had been carefully wrapped in plastic and ready to shoot – and then I got a call from Stan. He said, 'Are you sitting down? You might want to sit down. Because we may be changing these into a more humanoid look.' I was devastated. I thought they were so clever and so fun to look at – and they were *done*! I think Mr. Spielberg had some reservations

about them, but in the end he was won over by the idea and they remained in the film. I'm glad they did!"

Footage of the puppet Thermians interacting with the cast was seamlessly blended with blue-screen footage of the creatures. Originally, they were to get a couple more minutes' screen time but one of their scenes was cut. "In the scene where the young Thermian [Quellek] dies, he was originally going to lose it and turn 'full squid,'" says mechanical effects supervisor and tentacle puppeteer Christian Colquhoun. "We tried doing it with this special laying-down squid that had been designed for the scene while the actor [Patrick Breen] stood off to the side. But Dean was like, 'I'm not quite sure what's

Left to right: Two of Jordu Schell's Thermian concepts; sketch by Christopher Swift; a scarier concept by Berni Wrightson.

Copyright © 1999 Stan Winston Studio

going on here. I'm not getting the emotion. I'm not getting the pathos. So we're going to do it with the actor.' Everyone was like, aw! But I think it was a good choice. The squid looked great but it was hard to connect with it [in the scene]."

The other Thermian-related challenge during filming was the puppets' weight – perhaps inevitable given that they had to house large servos and pulleys, fiberglass body-support structures, and solid silicone bodies. "They were a little hard to puppeteer," remembers Colquhoun. "The silicone skins were really heavy because if they were any thinner, you'd have seen the ridges of the mechanism underneath."

"The heaviness of the silicone was a big deal," Landon agrees. "The Thermian on Sarris's torture table weighed so much, we had a heck of a time getting enough energy and explosive action out of it when it was shot. I think in post they [enhanced it] a little bit to make it look a little more violent than we were able to get on set."

For all of the puppeteering challenges, schedule rug-pulls, and near-cancellation, the Thermians emerged as one of the great creatures of '90s genre cinema, despite having only around five minutes of screen time. Writer Robert Gordon for one was delighted to see how his vaguely outlined creations had been realized on screen. "It was like a weird mind meld," he says. "I used to have Topps Ugly cards posted all over my wall, and even though I'd just described the Thermians as having tentacles or whatever, in my mind I'd always pictured this one Topps Ugly card named Bob. And the Thermians [on screen] was like the spirit of Bob come to life! It was so perfect." ✦

LAUGHTER OF THE TENTACLE

Both Christian Colquhoun and Richard Landon were on insert tentacle duties during the scene in which Fred and Lalieri make out while Guy looks on in horror. Colquhoun performed the "top tentacle" (also nicknamed "the Spoon") that pushes Fred down before looking up at Guy quizzically. "There were six of us puppeteering the tentacles just out of frame, and we were watching the actors and ourselves on monitors to judge where we were in the space," he says. "I remember Tony Shalhoub and Missi Pyle were so funny. And oh my God, Sam Rockwell! He was improvising like crazy and so good."

Landon agrees. "Sam Rockwell was ad-libbing all his lines, going totally off-script. 'Geez, get an aquarium!' 'What's wrong with you?' 'Where's that liquid even coming from?' It was a huge moment that made us all feel like we were working on this great thing together. It also telegraphed how fun the movie was going to be for the audience. Though it's hard to concentrate on not hitting an actor in the face with a big rubber tentacle when someone's throwing out all these hysterical one-liners behind you!"

SARRIS
AND THE FATU-KREY

As *Galaxy Quest*'s big bad, the late Robin Sachs was fitted with
experimental mechanical makeup that reacted to his facial expressions.

I N HIS MOVIEMAKING GUIDE, *BAMBI vs. Godzilla*, David Mamet famously described *Galaxy Quest* as a "perfect" movie. A small part of that may be down to Mamet's own influence on the movie – not least its bad guy. "I'd seen *The Untouchables* [scripted by Mamet] a million times, and it has such a great bad guy," says Robert Gordon. "I wanted Sarris to be just as bad as Al Capone was in that film."

As Mamet had done with Capone in *The Untouchables*, Gordon wanted the audience to discern Roth'h'ar Sarris's warped mindset from his deeds. Going down the *Spaceballs* route of having a bad guy played for laughs wasn't an option; Sarris needed to be someone you believed would inspire terror in the Thermians. "I felt that Sarris had to be the straight man, like Jason," Gordon says. "I didn't want a complex personality or a gregarious character that would take over. You had to really hate him. It was never filmed, but in my initial draft one of the things he does is beat Jason mercilessly down a hallway [filled with] captured Thermians to show them Jason is not who they thought he was."

The terror-inspiring General Roth'h'ar Sarris (Robin Sachs) with his lieutenant Lathe (Wayne Péré) and a Fatu-Krey guard.

Besides Capone, Gordon drew on one of *Star Trek*'s most famous villains. "Even though he really doesn't feel like Khan, I wanted it to come off as personal between Sarris and the Thermians [like Khan and Kirk in *Star Trek II: The Wrath of Khan*]. And I remember it was very important for Dean to show what was left of the Thermians' planet [after Sarris decimated it]."

In Gordon's script, Jason disparagingly refers to Sarris as "lobster head." Dean Parisot – working with costume designer Albert Wolsky – ran with the idea, realizing that the lobsterlike Sarris would make a great counter to the softer, squidlike Thermians, while tying into a theme of aquatic aliens. Keen for the villain to have some form of articulation, executive producer Steven Spielberg suggested passing Sarris's head and hands to the effects wizards at Stan Winston Studio, while the armor was a collaboration between the studio and Wolsky's costume department.

Sarris's articulation went far beyond what Parisot and Spielberg could have expected, thanks to groundbreaking mechanical technology created by Stan Winston Studio for a slated remake of *The Planet of the Apes* in the 1990s. On the latter project, Winston had tasked mechanical effects supervisor Christian Colquhoun with inventing a mechanical makeup that was driven by the actor's face and lips rather than being cable- or radio-controlled. His

Photo and McCreery, Barlowe and Wrightson concepts. Copyright © 1999 Stan Winston Studio

Sarris illustrations (left to right) by Crash McCreery, Wayne Barlowe, Gina DeDomenico, and Berni Wrightson. Main image: Key artist Scott Stoddard at work on the head sculpt. Opposite: Fatu-Krey soldier suit created by the costume department, and test of the clay-molded face and armor at Stan Winston Studio.

brief had been something of an engineering challenge, since it was notoriously difficult to get lips to move convincingly on large prosthetics makeup. "I developed a mouthpiece that you put in, which was basically like a retainer," Colquhoun says. "It had cables that were driven by the actor's lips, and there were three points of contact so you could push it in or pull it out to create different expressions."

Unfortunately for Stan Winston Studio, the effects on *The Planet of the Apes* ultimately went to Rick Baker; the movie was eventually released to middling reviews in 2001. However, Winston was keen that the nine months they had spent developing the technology would not be wasted. "When *Galaxy Quest* came around, Stan was like, 'We should totally do that with Sarris!'" Colquhoun says. "So, I was in charge of the mechanical makeup."

The final look of Sarris was designed by Christopher Swift (with refinements by Scott Stoddard), who sculpted the villain's head based on a lifecast of actor Robin Sachs. This was then coated in foam rubber. Colquhoun's mouth mechanics had to fit inside the head – but it wasn't as straightforward as simply transporting his nifty mouthpiece from ape head to alien head. "The ape head was pretty much like a human head. There was a wide flat area so that when the [mouthpiece] pushed out it separated [the lips]. Sarris had a different look that made it challenging to work as well as it did on *Apes*. It took a little time to figure out the thickness of the mold, because to get it to articulate the way you want it to, you had to [co-ordinate the mechanics with] the creases on the face. Chris [Swift] and I kind of fought a little bit about the makeup design. So it was challenging – but in the end it worked out really well."

The mechanical headpiece was topped with moving mechanical crab legs designed by Matt Heimlich, and a radio-controlled eyepatch. According to Colquhoun, the eyepatch was designed to lift up to reveal a semi-mechanical eye. However, the effect was not deployed in the final film as Dean Parisot remained unconvinced by the idea. One effect that was utilized was Sarris's RC-controlled, lobsterlike claw, which was puppeteered by Colquhoun.

BUILDING THE ARMOR

The designs for Sarris's head and claw were sent to Albert Wolsky's costume department so they could work up the rest of his costume. Costume illustrator Gina DeDomenico was tasked with visualizing costume concepts. "Albert gave me a book on crustaceans and shellfish as the inspiration for the character," she says. "We conceptualized insanely detailed armor that looked like something you might see underneath a boat. But Albert needed to figure out how the parts could actually move properly, and in the end it turned out a little more like traditional armor."

Once Wolsky and DeDomenico's refined design for the armor had been approved, the pieces were molded by special effects supervisor Matt Sweeney and sent to the costume's textile department to paint and add texture. However, Spielberg wanted the armor to articulate, too – at which point the armor became a joint project between the costume department and Stan Winston Studio. "We had to marry our departments," says costume supervisor Robert Q. Mathews. "We were working with the Stan Winston guys to put the pieces on the actor and see how everything came together, and our brilliant textile artist Matt Reitsma set up shop over there to paint the pieces they were

Guard costume photo courtesy of Prop Store. Sarris photo: Copyright © 1999 Stan Winston Studio

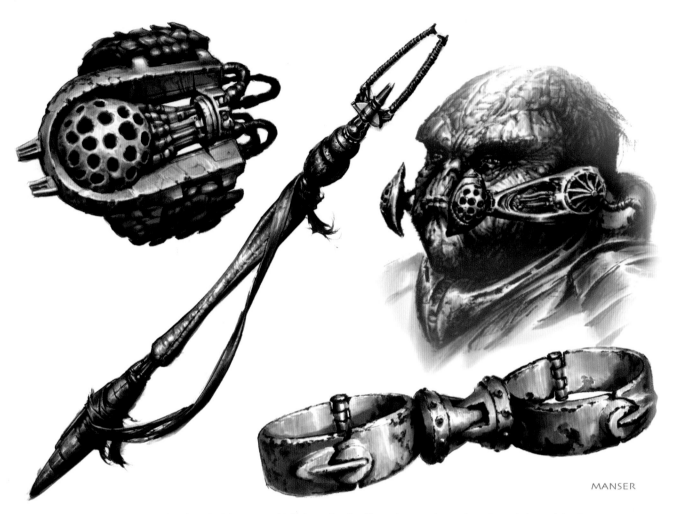

MANSER

Warren Manser's production illustration shows Sarris's "transport chief," along with a Fatu-Krey voice transmitter, cattle prod-type device, and shackles.

generating. Getting to interact with the Stan Winston guys was a great part of the job, because it was a whole different approach to costume making."

Stan Winston Studio's additions to the armor included cable-operated wings that burst out when the character got *really* angry, which were puppeteered by makeup department head Ve Neill (who also applied Robin Sachs's makeup). Cable-operated air bellows were fitted inside the suit, moving the shoulderplates and chestplates to simulate the effect of breathing.

Stan Winston Studio also created a simplified version of Sarris's mechanical makeup and armor for Sarris's lieutenant Lathe (played by Wayne Péré), including a crab-shaped urethane breastplate. The design for the remainder of the Fatu-Krey guards fell to the costume department. It would have been easy to give all of the guards a uniform style – but Wolsky didn't want to go down the easy route. "Albert wanted them to have their own individual look," says Mathews. "He designed about 10 different plastic shapes that could easily be made on a vacuform machine. They were shaped like

an abalone shell or a clamshell or a mussel shell. Then the textile people would use papier-mâché and different compounds to give the thin plastic pieces more texture and color, and we would use a tagger-gun to attach the shapes to the coveralls. They were really time-consuming. And then we had to maintain them through the course of shooting because they weren't terribly durable."

Another part of Sarris's guards that needed constant maintenance were the spaghettilike pieces draped over their heads. "That stuff had to be made on a daily basis because its shelf life was really, really short," Mathews laughs. "It was like pieces of tattered cloth made from a latex compound, and it was pretty fragile. Every time you took a piece of the costume off, the spaghetti stuff would start to fall apart. We had our workroom constantly making more batches of the stuff."

Not that any of this was any kind of horrific ordeal, Mathews points out. "It was a very rewarding experience. We had never created anything like this armor before and were learning as we went. God, it was fun!" ✦

Copyright © 1999 Stan Winston Studio

ROBIN SACHS

Dean Parisot had originally envisioned Tim Curry for the part of Sarris. Yet after Curry's experience on *Legend*, the actor was loath to wear elaborate prosthetics ever again. Instead, the role fell to the late Robin Sachs.

Curry's fears that the prosthetics would be agonizing to wear were not unfounded. The makeup took four hours to apply, while the latex and electronics made the suit extraordinarily hot and heavy. "Boy, Robin was a trouper," says Colquhoun. "They stuck glue to the outside of his face and glued these little things with dentures and magnets on the inside of his lips. And the set was all misty and wet. He was sweating like a horse, and the latex would soak up all the water. It would get even heavier and not operate so well. And then they waited until the end of the day to shoot him every time!"

Yet as Dean Parisot makes clear, Sachs never flew into a Sarris-like fury about the ordeal. "Robin was an incredibly good sport," says the director. "It took hours to get him ready, and that crap we put on him weighed 80 pounds! We had to give him a special chair to sit in. But he was the sweetest guy in the world and never complained once. Robin had that incredible voice, and he had the ability to play Sarris's insecurity and susceptibility to his own ego, as well as his rage."

While Sarris's role may have been the "straight man," Sachs was nevertheless a master of deadpan silliness. Robert Gordon remembers a few of Sachs's deranged takes on Sarris's initial ultimatum to Jason. "Robin performed the 'blood and pain' speech with various shadings among the takes. Sometimes with fury, sometimes with softer menace, but always with threat and intensity. Then it got sillier – but with Robin remaining in character as Sarris. 'First I require the Omega 13. Second, I require a small can of beans and a large opener.' On a subsequent take, things became musical. 'First, I require the Omega 13. Second, I would like to perform a ditty or two – pardon the lack of umbrella...' At which point he launched into a few bars of 'Singin' in the Rain.' He even performed a little dance as Sarris!"

DEMON BABIES

The fanged denizens of the mining colony were realized with the
help of dozens of artists, cutting-edge CGI, and rubber stand-ins.

THE ADORABLE BUT BLOODTHIRSTY aliens that toil at the mining outpost on the Crystal Planet were inspired by adorable but bloodthirsty creatures in another science fiction classic. "I was thinking of the doll scene from *Barbarella*," says Robert Gordon, referring to the delirious sequence in Roger Vadim's movie in which feral children tie up the heroine before unleashing fanged dolls to feast on Barbarella's flesh. "Originally, it went a bit too far [in the early drafts]. In one version, I established the blue babies as cannibals by having them slice thin pieces off a shoulder and eat them…"

Above: The demon babies turn from cute to killers. Opposite, top right: Paul Mejias sculpts the demon baby maquette, working from Berni Wrightson's design.

Copyright © 1999 Stan Winston Studio

CG artist Doug Sutton refined crowd software used in *Star Wars Episode I: The Phantom Menace* to help animate multiple demons running through frame.

BRINGING UP BABIES

The creation of the demon babies (dubbed "blue demons" in early drafts and the "Bokt" in Michael and Denise Okuda's Blu-ray *Galactopedia*) was a true collaboration between ILM and Stan Winston Studio. Under the supervision of art director Crash McCreery, Stan Winston Studio was responsible for creating the final design, while ILM was tasked with realizing it with CGI, as well as submitting additional concept ideas.

"The babies were difficult because you had to strike that balance between infantile and adorable, like puppies, and menacing," says ILM's VFX producer Kim Bromley. "There was a lot of back and forth between our art department and Stan Winston's guys, though the [final] design mostly came from them."

CONCEPT DESIGN GALLERY

Clockwise across both pages from right:
Two concepts by Stan Winston Studio's
Scott Stoddard; head color pattern concept
by Alex Jaeger; early concept by Simon
Bisley; two of Berni Wrightson's influential
designs; Kirk Henderson's reworked photo
of Erich Rigling's son; rear body color
concept by Jaeger; two childlike demon
faces by Henderson; Henderson's art
of the demons clutching severed hands;
Henderson's drawing of Jason captured
by the demons.

Copyright © 1999 Stan Winston Studio

"GALAXY QUEST"
BLUE DEMON ALIENS

Galaxy
Quest
1999

S. Bisley

Copyright © 1999 Stan Winston Studio

WRIGHTSON

Copyright © 1999 Stan Winston Studio

A demon baby unwinds in between takes; VFX producer Robert Stadd in Goblin Valley with two rubber demon babies that were used to plan out effects shots.

Artists at both studios came up with wildly different takes on the creatures. "My designs looked more reptilian," recalls Simon Bisley. "They had frills like dinosaurs and some of them had plates that curved up like on a triceratops. They also had horns and were more tribal-looking."

ILM's Kirk Henderson also created several "tribal" looking designs. "I was told they would have tattoos all over their body," he recalls. "I was also told they were going to be bald with a little bit of red hair on the top, and then I was told to make it so you could see their skulls through their skin when they snarled. That all changed."

Henderson also worked up a variety of realistic facial expressions (both cute and menacing) for the demons by Photoshopping pictures of concept designer Erich Rigling's son. Webbed feet, sharp teeth,

and a bald head were added to the photos, and Henderson also experimented with different skin tones and eye colors. "He turned my son into an alien baby!" laughs Rigling. "That was a bit disturbing."

Even more disturbing was Henderson's concept art based on Gordon's initial, more bloodthirsty take on the sequence. "I was asked to create devices that could be used for cannibalism," he recalls. "One device I created was this 'cheese-grater' that you could rake across someone to get layers of skin. It was pretty disgusting!"

MINER THREAT

The final, shark-toothed demon baby design was drawn by legendary horror-comic artist Berni Wrightson. This was used as the basis for an initial maquette sculpted by Stan Winston Studio artist Paul

The demon babies appear concerned by an injured colleague – only to pounce and tear him apart. The sequence was originally more gruesome.

Mejias. This in turn provided the foundation for the final CG model, which was free-sculpted by ILM's top creature modeler, Geoff Campbell. Campbell made several further changes to Wrightson's design, adding bigger, constantly twitching ears and making the babies appear pudgier and cuter. Henderson's Photoshopped pictures of Rigling's son provided Campbell with useful reference for these changes.

As in Robert Gordon's script and Kirk Henderson's early illustrations, the CG sequence was initially much more violent. "We did some animation where they were ripping another lot [of demon babies] apart that was really horrific and very funny," says ILM's VFX supervisor Bill George. "But when the studio wanted to move more toward a kid-friendly audience, we needed to tone it down."

Several full-size rubber demon babies were also constructed and brought to the Goblin Valley shoot. These were vital in giving the CGI team lighting reference that they could match in postproduction, as well as giving an idea of how much space the sadistic miners would take up in shots. The rubber versions proved useful stand-ins during filming. "You need something to react to, so I was always using surrogates," says Dean Parisot. "I still have a rubber blue baby sitting in my office!" ✦

Above: ILM did CG color tests on a scan of the sculpt. Right: Miles Teves's killer plant.

KILLER PLANTS

There are a variety of ways to die on the Crystal Planet: eaten by demon babies, crushed by Gorignak, trampled by a pig lizard. In early versions of the story there was one more. At one point, the heroes had to trek through a field of flesh-eating plants to reach the mine, and ILM concept artists Erich Rigling and Miles Teves worked up ideas as to what the plants might look like. "I was thinking a bit about Triffids and of Amazonian swamp flowers that dissolve their victims with acid," says Teves. Sadly, the plants never made it beyond the concept stage and were dropped from the movie.

Copyright © 1999 Stan Winston Studio

Stan Winston Studio key effects artists Trevor Hensley and Rob Ramsdell add details to the pig lizard sculpt prior to painting.

PIG LIZARD

To play the pig lizard, Shane Mahan needed to master walking in a
hunched position while viewing a topsy-turvy world in a pocket mirror.

ROBERT GORDON DIDN'T NEED TO write a long, detailed description of the first monster that confronts Jason on the mining colony. Two beautifully simple words sufficed: pig lizard. "I felt like I had this power where I could write these strange, specific things like 'pig lizard' and they'd come to life," Gordon laughs. "I mean, it didn't have to be a pig lizard. It could have been a giraffe donkey."

Gordon's script did provide two small additional facts about the pig lizard: it had a big tongue and a lot of teeth. Beyond that, it was down to the artists at Stan Winston Studio to figure out what a pig

lizard actually looked like. As with all of *Galaxy Quest*'s creatures, multiple artists worked up dozens of wildly different concepts. Some looked piggier or more lizardlike than others. Ultimately, it was Crash McCreery's design that received the mark of approval. McCreery's illustration depicted the creature as a squat, fleshy, and deliriously ugly brute, but crucially it also outlined how a performer could practically operate the monster.

"I knew it was going to be a guy in a suit so I made it bipedal, and I pulled from the work we'd done on *Jurassic Park* in terms of skin textures and anatomy," says McCreery. "But just the term 'pig lizard'

The final pig lizard suit had multiple eyes, a mouthful of jagged teeth, and fleshy protrusions.

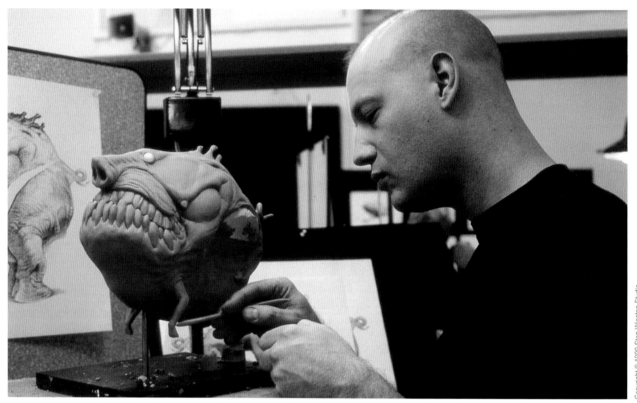

Copyright © 1999 Stan Winston Studio

Sculptor Greg Figiel puts the finishing touches to the pig lizard maquette.

Copyright © 1999 Stan Winston Studio

One of Crash McCreery's pig lizard concepts.

– in my mind, I kind of immediately knew what that could look like. It was just a matter of making it look more alien. We knew we wanted to have a giant mouth, and then we added more eyes to the creature."

There was just one thing left to decide: who was going to climb inside the pig lizard costume. There weren't many volunteers. Eventually, character effects supervisor Shane Mahan piped up. "Foolishly, I said to Stan, 'Well, I'm going to be out there anyway so why don't I just play this thing?'" Mahan remembers. "Stan said, 'That's a great idea!' So I ended up with the distinctive honor of being the pig lizard."

ROASTED PIG

The pig lizard suit was constructed predominantly from foam latex and fiberglass, and was fitted with a silicon tongue. Mahan needed to work closely with the creature's animatronic supervisor, Rich Haugen, to determine the weight distribution of its mechanics, as well as practical details, like the best way

Jason is confronted by the pig lizard (performed by Shane Mahan). Above right: Mahan "relaxes" by hanging on an A-frame and being blasted by a hairdryer.

Above: Crash McCreery's final design, showing how the suit would be worn.
Below: Pencil drawing by Stan Winston Studio artist Jim Charmatz.

Above: ILM's Kirk Henderson worked up several concepts during preproduction.

Copyright © 1999 Stan Winston Studio

Copyright © 1999 Stan Winston Studio

to get in and out of the suit. "There was a zipper on the bum of the thing and that was the only way in," Mahan says. "I had to crawl up the bum and put my legs in. I also had an extraordinarily heavy chestpiece sewn to my vest. They would bolt me through the top of that so it would be secure. It was quite an operation."

Moving inside the pig lizard suit was no easy feat, either. The suit required Mahan to walk in a squat, hunched-over position, and it took hours of practice to perfect its bouncy gait, especially as he needed to simultaneously operate the jaw and tongue movements using his arms.

Filming the sequence in the excruciating heat of Goblin Valley made the job even more challenging. Because it was such an arduous process to get in and out of the suit, Mahan stayed inside for hours at a time – though he did get to enjoy the occasional break several feet up in the air. "The guys would hook me up to an A-frame winch and I would hang there like a caught shark on the dock. The winch took all the weight off it, and I could relax in midair between shots. There was also a Velcro tab in the belly of the costume that I could open up to get air."

A tiny camera was installed inside one of the teeth so Mahan could see where he was going during filming. "I could shift between the camera feed, where I could see Tim Allen coming toward me, and my own sight," Mahan recalls. "But what happened on day three or four is it got so hot that the camera mechanism burned out and the technician couldn't activate it again. So Stan, with his quick thinking, went up to a makeup girl and asked for her pocket mirror. Then he wedged this three-inch pocket mirror inside [the suit] so I could see the world upside down. For the rest of the shoot, I would look in that mirror, that's how I got around. It was like an upside-down periscope with only one view." Sometimes Mahan had to rely on sound to decipher what was happening to him. "During the fight, real rocks were thrown at me and I could just hear these big, heavy hits," he says. "The pig lizard suffered through some abusive moments!"

Despite the extreme discomfort of wearing the suit, Mahan stresses that the entire shoot was a blast. "We just had a laugh out there," he says. "It was enormously satisfying. The pig lizard should have had his own movie!"

So having gotten so close to the pig lizard during filming, how did Mahan feel about the creature's gruesome end in the digital conveyor? "Oh, that was a lot of fun too," he laughs. "It was a separate puppet that we rigged to squirt fluids and shimmy and shake as it turned inside out. Luckily, I was not inside that one...." ✦

Mahan's visibility was severely limited inside the pig lizard suit – especially after a camera mechanism burned out.

Rock monster concept by science fiction artist Wayne Barlowe. The creature had clearly defined facial features in many early illustrations.

Copyright © 1999 Stan Winston Studio

GORIGNAK

Galaxy Quest's towering rock star was brought to life through groundbreaking lighting and animation tools. Yet he was almost cut from the movie completely…

PERSISTENT SUGGESTIONS THAT Gorignak is a homage to *Star Trek V*'s infamously abandoned rockman scene may be way off the mark, but the sequence did have *Trek* in its DNA. "I don't even think I'd seen that [*Star Trek V* sequence] so I wasn't consciously referencing it," says Robert Gordon. "But I was thinking about other rocklike monsters that had been in *Star Trek* as well as *The Neverending Story*. And, of course, the scene references

[*Star Trek* episode] 'Arena.' 'Can you fashion some sort of rudimentary lathe?' is a play on the idea that Kirk has somehow found time to make this cannon out of diamonds!"

Gordon's giant rock monster was initially described as having an ominous, though largely featureless, face. During the film's early conceptual stages, ILM, Stan Winston Studio, and the production art departments all submitted illustrations that ran with the idea of a humanoid rock man with some kind of face. "I drew a big rock

Creating the rock monster involved refining software to combine creature animation with real-world physics.

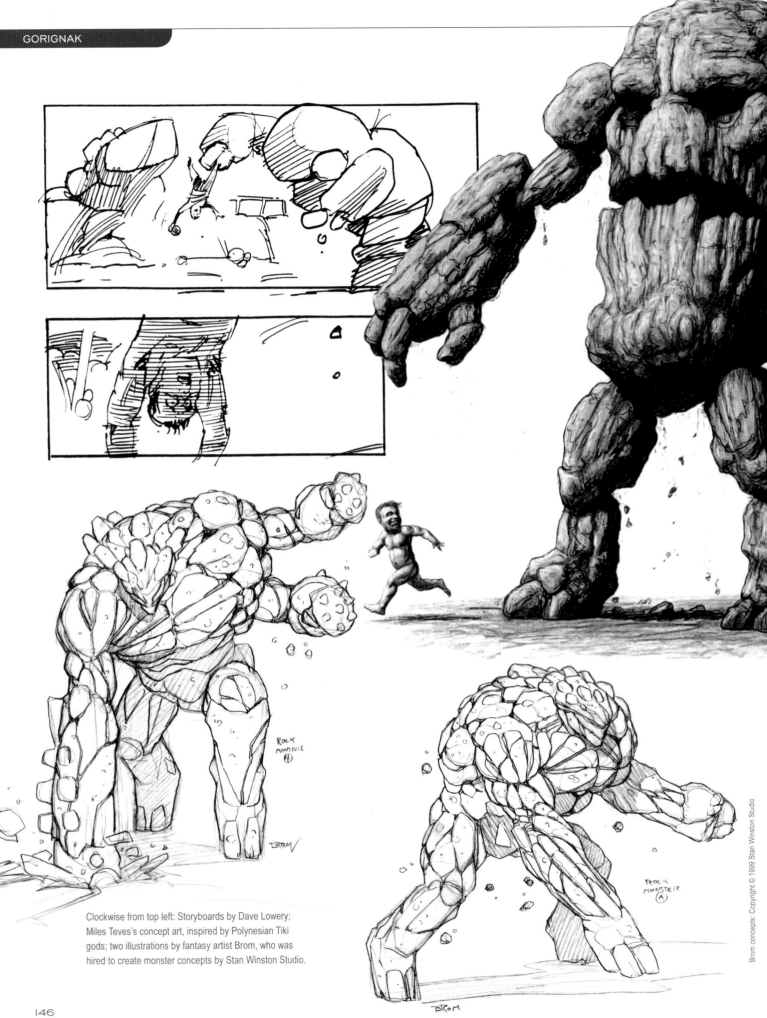

Clockwise from top left: Storyboards by Dave Lowery; Miles Teves's concept art, inspired by Polynesian Tiki gods; two illustrations by fantasy artist Brom, who was hired to create monster concepts by Stan Winston Studio.

Brom concepts: Copyright © 1999 Stan Winston Studio

man disguised in the mountain landscape," recalls Stan Winston Studio artist Simon Bisley. "It was distorted, big, and cumbersome and had foliage hanging off him. I did one drawing with a house on his back… He was like a deformed King Kong made of rock. They didn't use any of it."

The concept of the rock monster gradually moved from a creature with a recognizable face to something rather more abstract. It was ILM's visual effects supervisor, Bill George, who decided to take it in a different direction. "My idea was that the rocks are not actually the monster, but it's actually some sort of electrical field that is alive and puts things together to create a body so it can move around," he explains. "So we didn't want a face or eyes. We wanted it to be able to assemble itself, fall apart, and come back together."

Visual effects art director Alex Jaeger and concept designer Erich Rigling worked up new designs based on George's idea, which were eventually turned into a rock-based maquette. "We discussed its ephemeral nature and how it could remodel and reform itself down the hallway after it crashed through walls," says Rigling. "The concept evolved as it went from the writer to one artist to another artist. Everyone's ideas came together to create something unique."

Unlike *Star Trek V*'s rockman, Gorignak would be brought to life with CGI rather than a rubber suit and smoke. But before ILM could begin figuring out how to animate their rock monster concept, a problem arose: the studio wanted the creature excised from the movie. Second unit director Stefen Fangmeier – who was VFX co-supervisor on the movie during preproduction while Harold Ramis was still attached – recalls this being an edict early on. "I remember having arguments with the studio because they wanted to cut the rock monster, which was my favorite character," he says. "I said, 'You can't get rid of the rock monster – it's way too funny!'"

The requests to cut the sequence didn't disappear once Dean Parisot took the reins. So how did Parisot manage to fight off these

Concept art of Gorignak on the mining planet by Randy Gaul.

demands? By simply ignoring them, apparently. "Dean's style is to say, 'You want to cut the rock monster? Yes, OK' – and then not do it!" laughs Gordon. "Then later he'd get another note: 'I told you to cut the rock monster!' And he'd say, 'Absolutely' – and still wouldn't do it!"

SCHOOL OF ROCK

Creating a monster like Gorignak with CGI was not straightforward in 1999. Unlike more fantastical creatures, it had to believably simulate the way real boulders looked and moved, while its interaction with the brightly lit, desert environment – as well as the live-action footage of Tim Allen – was difficult to pull off convincingly. To make matters even trickier, the tight schedule meant there was no time for extensive testing.

Thankfully, new animation tools developed by ILM's technical supervisor James Tooley and software developer Jim Hourihan made the process much easier. Associate visual effects supervisor Ben Snow remembers how the tools helped combine creature

animation and real-world physics in new ways. "The idea was that the character could be a fully animated, limbed creature with an apparent skeleton like a regular creature, but then we could dial in the contribution of the animation. So, we could go from a physics-based simulation of rolling boulders that were attracted together to form the creature, to having a full animated character, to then having the creature hit a wall and go back to being a physics simulation of exploding rocks."

The rock monster animation itself was created by sequence supervisor Ed Kramer and animator Scott Wirtz, using the 3D graphics application, Softimage. Their work was enhanced by footage of dust particles and rock debris (seen falling off the rock monster as it charges through the desert and the corridors of the *Protector*), which were shot by Bill George and co-visual effects supervisor Ed Hirsh. "We'd study the animation of the rock monster and then shoot people on the backlot dropping red sand to match it," recalls Snow. "The compositors would then track all that in."

GALAXY QUEST #25
WM COLITSON

Rock monster concept illustration by seminal comic book artist Berni Wrightson.

Copyright © 1999 Stan Winston Studio

The rock monster on the rampage; Gorignak is blasted into space. In Gordon's original draft, Gorignak's silent roar was subtitled "Ah, sweet tranquility at last."

Extensive CG work was also needed for Gorignak's interaction with the interiors of the *Protector*. Enhancements included digital dents in corridor walls and a CG door wrenched open by the rampaging creature. Meanwhile, a digital Jason was created for the moment in which the *Protector*'s commander is tossed about by Gorignak, which was tracked to live-action footage of a stuntman pulling Tim Allen along and the actor suspended on wires.

Like the demon babies, another significant challenge was how to light the sequence. Snow remembers ILM trying to figure out a way to light Gorignak that would accurately reflect both the sun's illumination and the indirect illumination from rays bouncing off other surfaces. "We were picking our brains wondering, 'How are we going to do this?'" Snow says. "The ambient light tools we had at the time were really unsatisfactory in terms of the colors. In the end we used a big array of smaller lights, which was something I learned

from [visual effects director of photography] Pat Sweeney as a way to make a model spaceship feel inherently bigger. We also used a new lighting tool called Irender, which replaced the clunky software we'd used on previous films and became ILM's main CG lighting tool for years after *Galaxy Quest*. It made the lighting process much quicker and made it possible to do the elaborate lighting rigs that the rock monster needed."

While the stone-faced behemoth at the center of these lighting and animation breakthroughs is largely seen stomping, smashing, and clobbering its way through *Galaxy Quest*, the final shot of the creature is much more serene – the result of a concept perhaps not entirely apparent in the final movie. "There was this whole idea that the rock monster hated sound," says concept designer Alex Jaeger. "That's why when he eventually gets shot into space, he relaxes. He's like, 'Ah, finally – silence!'" ✦

THE MAK'TAR

The Mak'tar headpiece worn by Alan Rickman had to be
old-fashioned and slightly crude without being preposterous.

Top right: Blood tick concept art by Warren Fu. Above: Rickman wearing the Mak'tar headpiece in the movie. The piece was based on a cast of the actor's head.

WE GLEAN A HANDFUL OF INTRIGUING facts about the Mak'tar in *Galaxy Quest*. They deploy the stealth haze to avoid capture. They can gain extra power through a communal chant of strength ("*Larak tarath*"). One of their favorite meals is Kep-mok blood ticks. They have a head adorned with ridges, frills, and indentations. And the death of a loved one will evoke the age-old oath, "By Grabthar's hammer, by the sons of Warvan, you will be avenged" – a "placeholder line" that ended up sticking, according to Robert Gordon.

Bearing in mind that little other information about the Mak'tar is made explicit, the headpiece worn by Alan Rickman had to appear serious enough to suggest great significance to the Thermians, iconic enough to appeal to the legion of *Galaxy Quest* fans, and unrefined enough to reflect the fact it hailed from a two-decade-old show. Stan Winston Studio's effects supervisor Shane Mahan, who sculpted the master headpiece based on one of Crash McCreery's designs, recalls the challenge in combining these conflicting ideas. "It was tricky, as it was supposed to look like late '70s/early '80s television show makeup where it was a little obvious and crude, yet it had to look cool enough on its own too," he says. "And Alan

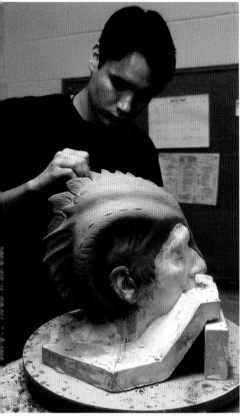

Left to right: Jason Matthews adds details to a headpiece sculpt; terrifying toilet design by Warren Manser; Alexander is forced to maintain his Dr. Lazarus guise.

Rickman didn't want it to look preposterously silly. He wanted the joke to work – that it was something that was once taken seriously and now is the bane of [Alexander's] existence."

As well as having his head cast for the piece, Rickman spent a day at the studio discussing ideas about the prosthetics and testing out how the designs worked for the character. "Alan had a particular idea about how he wanted his nose straightened out, and then he was quite happy with it," Mahan recalls. "Like, I totally understood. There's not one scene where he's not wearing this thing; it never came off! So we had to treat it with care."

WEAR AND TEAR

Multiple "hero" and distressed versions were made for Rickman to wear throughout the movie. Each headpiece was cast out of latex and polyfoam and attached to a foam rubber forehead and nose. The final headpiece design boasted enough detail and craftmanship to appear like something that could have genuinely come from the period, while maintaining a simple paint scheme and obvious seamlines to differentiate itself from modern prosthetics effects. "I kept wanting to make it better!" Mahan laughs. "I had to keep telling

myself, 'No, this needs to have some visual humor.'"

One of the movie's neat jokes is the way that the headpiece gradually deteriorates over the course of the film. Makeup department head Ve Neill was on hand to suggest ways in which it could tear and allow hair to roguishly poke through. The headpiece appeared in rejuvenated form in the TV revival at the end of the movie, and Neill dusted it with a pearlescent color to make it look slicker and more pristine. Neill was also in charge of applying Rickman's cosmetic makeup which had to complement the prosthetics. "I said to Stan, 'I think it should be slightly theatrical,'" Neill says. "And of course, we were going for that old-fashioned *Star Trek* feel. I used iridescent colors on his face and brought [the color] back onto the headpiece so it blended together."

Fans of the Mak'tar can find out more about the species in Michael and Denise Okuda's Blu-ray *Galactopedia*. It reveals that they are a "fundamentalist religious sect known for strict asceticism," and that Dr. Lazarus is a former philosopher who is the only survivor from planet Tev'Mek after it was decimated by Meechan invaders. A sequence cut from the movie also informs us that the Mak'tar sleep on a bed of spikes and use the galaxy's most terrifying toilet. ✦

Galaxy Quest's cosmic backdrops are brimming with alien worlds and starfields that
ILM realized through a combination of digital mattes and computer graphics.

THERMIA

Though it is never made explicit, the eaten-away planet
glimpsed beyond the *Protector* as it embarks on its maiden
voyage is the remnants of the Thermians' homeworld,
Thermia ("Theramin" in Gordon's original draft).

"It went through a bunch of iterations," remembers
concept designer Erich Rigling. "I did a couple of designs
of it as a floating technological city that went nowhere.
Then we came up with the idea that it was the wreckage
of the Thermians' homeworld which had a bunch of cities
built onto the underside of the crust. It's like a broken
husk of a planet. They're clinging on to it for dear life and
building on it with manufactured parts." The final digital
matte painting of Thermia was created by Randy Gaul.

THE CRYSTAL PLANET

The establishing shot of the mining planet (referred to as the Crystal
Planet in Gordon's early drafts and Epsilon Gorniar II in the Blu-ray
Galactopedia) was a digital matte based on concept art by Alex Jaeger.

Mattes by artists including Ronn Brown and Jett Green were also
used to enhance scenes that were filmed at Goblin Valley. "We created
multiple looks for the planet's skies for the director to choose," explains
Brown. "They needed to be alien-looking, twisterlike skies that were
not too busy to take attention from the characters. We started with
photos that we took ourselves or from the location photographer.
Then we drew on them digitally using Photoshop and After Effects to
give the clouds slight movement. Many of the planet's landscapes are
a combination of footage shot on location and matte paintings that
extended shots or made slight rock and landscape changes."

SKY/MINE EXTENSION
CP-11 #2
GALAXY QUEST
CONCEPT ART
© ILM ART DEPT
7/1/99   A. JAEGER

STARFIELDS

"Putting the Milky Way in a movie was something I'd always wanted to do – and on *Galaxy Quest* I finally got to do it!" says ILM's VFX supervisor Bill George. "The denser line of stars was used as a compositional piece so it complemented what the ship was doing. So if the ship came in from one side, we'd add the starfield in a diagonal position."

The starfields (including "retro" fields for the *Galaxy Quest* TV series) were generated using software written by associate VFX supervisor Ben Snow, who was inspired by stars in other shows. "I did a lot of analysis," says Snow. "Our favorite stars were from *The Empire Strikes Back*, which were done by practical means. *Star Trek* created starfields using matte paintings or sometimes poking holes in plastic. We wanted to render our stars really fine like that but had an obsession with them being as perfect as possible. I also added galaxies to the starfield."

PLANETS AND BLACK HOLES

When Jason gazes out of the window of the spaceport for the first time, he is dumbfounded to see alien worlds before him. Computer graphics supervisor Dan B Goldman was tasked with turning 2D concept art of the spacescape into a 3D image. "Bill George wanted to see some sort of motion so it didn't feel like it was just a painting," Goldman says. "There were a couple of planets in the background which were gently rotating, and the sun had flares coming off it."

Moments later in the scene, Jason is sucked into a swirling black hole (a phenomenon that later reoccurs when the *Protector*'s command module heads for Earth). The effect was created with another of Randy Gaul's digital mattes, which was augmented with CGI.

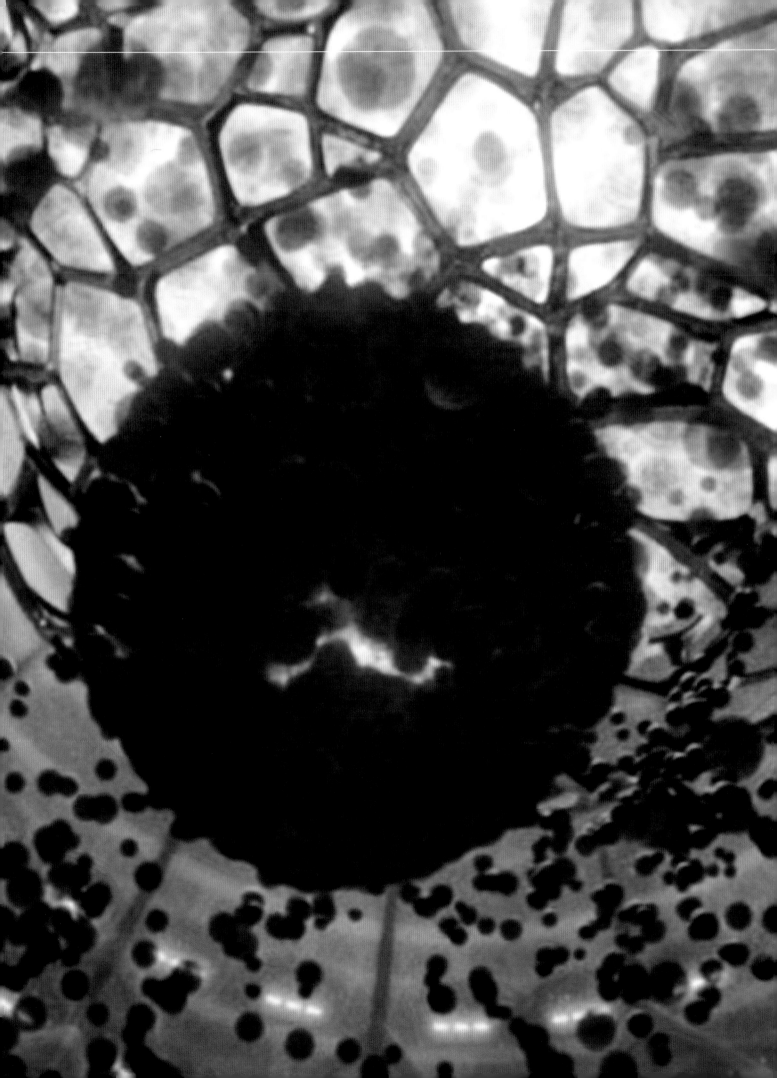

WEAPONS AND GADGETS

The tech deployed by both the Thermians and Fatu-Krey was largely designed
by concept artist Warren Manser and built by prop master Jerry Moss.

ION NEBULIZER

APPEARANCE GENERATOR

ION NEBULIZER

This phaser-like energy blaster is the Thermians' primary handheld weapon. Like all of the Thermians' tech, it is inspired by the *Galaxy Quest* TV show but boasts highly complex inner workings – as evidenced by the strange blue liquid that seeps out when one is crushed by the Chompers. In addition to the aluminum nebulizer props used in the movie's battle sequences (described by concept artist Warren Manser as "the best prop fabrications I had seen"), a simplified version appears in the clips of the original TV show. Meanwhile, toy replicas can be spotted in the convention scenes. An early draft of Robert Gordon's script names the weapons as "magneto-pistols," while David Howard's *Captain Starshine* script favors "disintegrators." Manser's concept art, meanwhile, dubs them "disruptors."

APPEARANCE GENERATOR

This piece of equipment is attached to the belt and allows the cephalopodlike Thermians to take on different forms, including human, in order to blend into other societies. The perils of forgetting to activate the generator are made apparent when the Thermians, in their true guise, arrive to greet the petrified *Galaxy Quest* cast. Sarris also uses one to disguise himself as Fred.

INTERSTELLAR VOX

CLIPBOARD   BINOCULARS

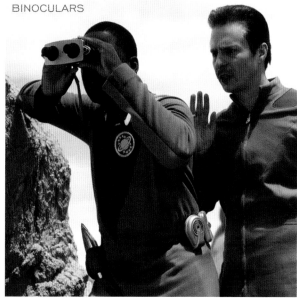

INTERSTELLAR VOX

The interstellar vox is almost like a space-age take on the mobile phone. Echoing *Star Trek*'s communicators, this enables the Thermians – and the human crew – to contact the ship or other members of a landing party while on alien worlds. Jason also uses one to keep in touch with Brandon. *Galaxy Quest* fans are seen eagerly clutching plastic replicas during the convention scenes.

DATA COLLECTION TOOLS

In a scene that didn't make it into the movie, a Thermian named Glath passes Jason a "situational analysis" on a high-tech clipboard – prompting Jason to autograph it before handing it back. Despite its name, the clipboard (briefly seen being clutched by Lahnk) more closely resembles a proto-iPad than an actual clipboard. Another data collection tool seen in the film is a pair of auto-telescoping, long-distance binoculars used on the Crystal Planet.

TRANSLATOR

SURFACE MAPPER

CLIPBOARD

ION SHIELD

ION SHIELD

This defensive shield can be clipped
to the belt. In a deleted scene, the
Thermian Neru is seen presenting
Tommy with one such device. Its
precise function is unknown. The
gadget is called a "valence shield" in
Robert Gordon's original script but
renamed an "ion shield" in the replica
props seen at the convention.

SURFACE MAPPER

Like an interstellar Google
Maps, this device is used by
the crew to locate a beryllium
sphere on the mining planet.
Tommy is unimpressed to
discover Alexander is holding
the gadget upside down. They
were sometimes referred to as
"'tricorders" by the props team.

TRANSLATOR

Echoing *Star Trek*'s universal
translator, this device allows
the Thermians to understand
other species and in turn be
understood. Without a working
translator, the Thermians' real
voice is an aural onslaught of
deranged yelping and gymnastic
tongue-rolls.

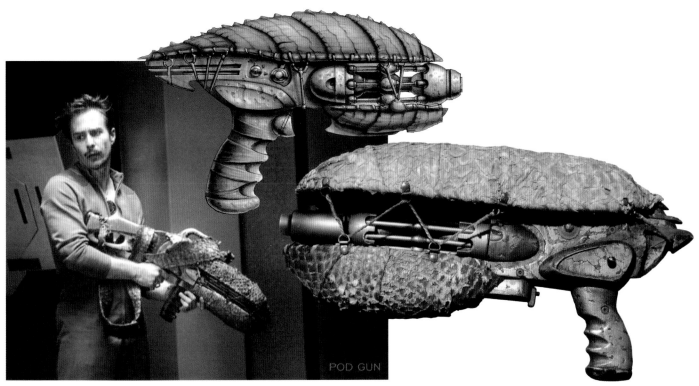

POD GUN

SARRIS'S KNIFE

MANSER

TORTURE DEVICE

POD GUNS

The pod guns deployed by the Fatu-Krey have a similar aesthetic to the species' starship and costumes. Green, organic-looking, bulky, and threatening, these weapons contrast with the sleek, silver weaponry of the Thermians. The final concept design was drawn by artist Wil Rees.

SARRIS'S KNIFE

In the third act of *Galaxy Quest*, Sarris disguises himself as Fred – only for Jason (having gone back in time after activating the Omega 13) to expose his true identity. Sarris proceeds to pull out a large, jagged, double-sided dagger somewhat resembling a Klingon blade.

TORTURE DEVICES

Two Thermians are seen strapped to Fatu-Krey torture devices. First, the *Galaxy Quest* cast watch in horror as Mathesar shows them a smuggled tape of the original Thermian leader's limbs being twisted and cracked in different directions by Sarris. Later, Mathesar is strapped to a table (a "tear harness" according to Sarris) and electrocuted by a cattle-prod device, briefly reverting him to cephalopod form. The latter effects were realized through a combination of Stan Winston Studio's puppetry and ILM's animated energy blasts.

GELEVATOR

The texture and consistency of the space-shooting blobs were worked
out through experiments with old photos and buckets of slime.

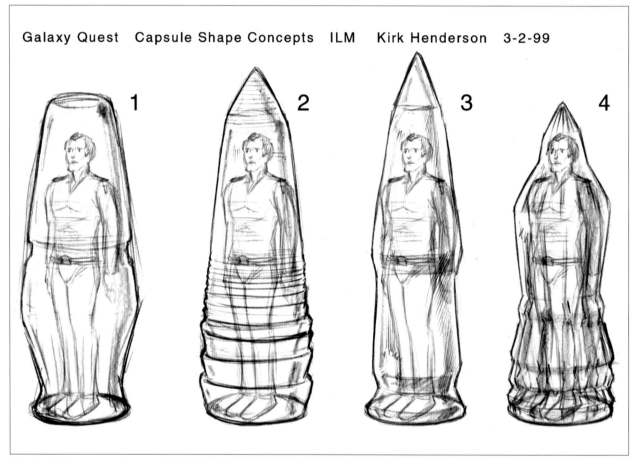

Galaxy Quest Capsule Shape Concepts ILM Kirk Henderson 3-2-99

1   2   3   4

ILM artist Kirk Henderson worked up 17 different capsule shapes that could transport the *Galaxy Quest* cast to the ship.

THERE ARE VARIOUS WAYS TO TRAVEL between Thermian spacecraft and *terra firma*: shuttle, digital conveyor, flying limo, the *Protector*'s command module... But perhaps the weirdest method of transport deployed for interstellar travel is the gelevator (or "Jell-O pod"): a protective bullet-shaped blob of goo that encases someone as they're shot across space into the pod bay.

ILM concept artist Kirk Henderson drew up over a dozen different shapes of pods that would encase the passenger to protect them from space during the light-speed journey. Once the bullet shape had been chosen, ILM needed to work out the texture for the goo. "We tried a lot of different things from Saran Wrap and cones to tubes and sorbet – all kinds of different weird materials," remembers concept designer Erich Rigling. "Because it was a comedy, we wanted it to look weird and interesting. We had worked on the film *Flubber*, and that gave us the idea of cocooning Jason in Jell-O."

To test the effectiveness of the goo concepts, Rigling experimented on a series of photographs of creative director Mark

Moore being disintegrated that had been worked up for *Mars Attacks!* "The final artwork was of Mark coated in Jell-O in space!"

To work out the exact nature of the digital goo, ILM's practical effects team mixed up six buckets containing different consistencies of methylcellulose, a thickening agent used in everything from shampoo to laxatives. "I put my hands into the buckets to feel them," says CG supervisor Dan B Goldman. "I was like, 'Oh, this one is cool, let's mix the bigger chunks from one bucket with the gloopier stuff from another bucket. We then shot film plates of the methylcellulose for some of the drips and globs coming off of the characters as they come out of the gelevator."

These drips were composited into the final digital goo, which was created by ILM's technical director, David Hisanaga. For the gelevator's initial appearance, the goo was wrapped around a CG model of Jason that was tracked to live-action footage of Tim Allen. The end result was, as Fred Kwan says, a hell of a thing. ✦

A digital model of Tim Allen was encased in CG goo and practical slime; storyboard panels by Collin Grant based on artwork by Kirk Henderson.

TOTHIAN MINES

The design of the magnetic mines was worked out in plastic
and paste before being rendered by ILM's Rebel Mac unit.

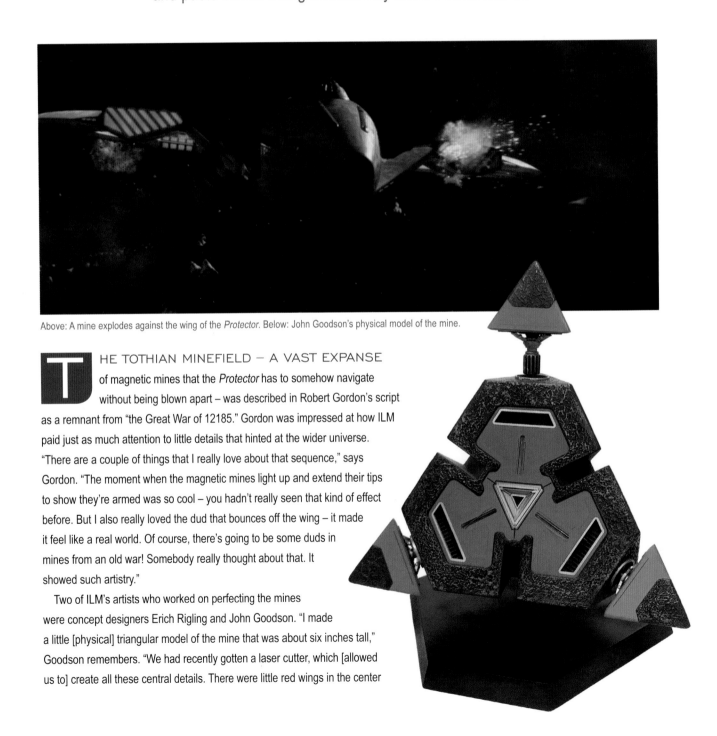

Above: A mine explodes against the wing of the *Protector*. Below: John Goodson's physical model of the mine.

THE TOTHIAN MINEFIELD — A VAST EXPANSE
of magnetic mines that the *Protector* has to somehow navigate
without being blown apart – was described in Robert Gordon's script
as a remnant from "the Great War of 12185." Gordon was impressed at how ILM
paid just as much attention to little details that hinted at the wider universe.
"There are a couple of things that I really love about that sequence," says
Gordon. "The moment when the magnetic mines light up and extend their tips
to show they're armed was so cool – you hadn't really seen that kind of effect
before. But I also really loved the dud that bounces off the wing – it made
it feel like a real world. Of course, there's going to be some duds in
mines from an old war! Somebody really thought about that. It
showed such artistry."

Two of ILM's artists who worked on perfecting the mines
were concept designers Erich Rigling and John Goodson. "I made
a little [physical] triangular model of the mine that was about six inches tall,"
Goodson remembers. "We had recently gotten a laser cutter, which [allowed
us to] create all these central details. There were little red wings in the center

of all three sides – fairly detailed inset pieces. The model was fabricated out of plastic and wood, and textured with modeling paste to give it a stucco texture."

ENTER THE REBELS

Once the physical model was approved, it was digitally recreated by ILM's Rebel Mac unit, who specialized in rendering CG spaceships with Macs. Using the 3D animation package ElectricImage, they were able to replicate all of the intricate details on Goodson's model for close-ups and create texture maps based on the model's paints and weathering effects. Crucially, they could duplicate a single mine so that thousands of the weapons could be seen extending into the distance.

"The other challenge was that the minefield was in a space cloud," adds Rebel Mac's then-supervisor Stu Maschwitz. "Rendering 3D fog – called 'volumetric' rendering – was at the very limit of ILM's rendering capabilities at the time, and something we'd developed for *Twister*. It was very render-intensive and hard to control. But in Rebel Mac we had access to an experimental feature in ElectricImage that could render sparse volumetric fog, so we used it for the scenes where the ships are flying through the cloud. It was an example of how we pushed right up against the edge of what was possible at the time". ✦

Early effects storyboards by Kirk Henderson show the mines as cube-shaped weapons.

Close-up of one bomb with the minefield stretching out into the distance. The CGI was created by ILM's Rebel Mac unit, who used ElectricImage to duplicate a single mine.

Jason and Gwen are confronted with the Chompers' final fiery flourish. The flames in this part of the sequence were shot separately and composited into the scene.

THE CHOMPERS

It's a prerequisite for any self-respecting spaceship:
a deadly gauntlet filled with colossal crushers and flame-jets….

"IT SERVES NO USEFUL PURPOSE for there to be a bunch of chompy, crushy things in the middle of a hallway!" While Gwen understandably isn't a big admirer of the Chompers, for many *Galaxy Quest* fans the death-defying gauntlet is one of the highlights of the movie (with or without Sigourney Weaver's F-bomb). Gordon remembers how the sequence was inspired by a deadly obstacle course in an earlier movie. "In Jerry Zucker's *First Knight,* there was a gauntlet scene in which Lancelot

must navigate a complex medieval mechanism chock-full of various hazards. I remember thinking that this kind of nightmare escalation would be perfect for a moment in which the writer of the *Galaxy Quest* TV show has scribbled a random challenge for the show's protagonists. And now it's been reconstructed in real life by the Thermians as an obstacle course for Gwen and Jason!"

While Gordon knew that timing would be paramount to the survival of the protagonists as they traversed the Chompers, he didn't want

The computer-generated Chompers were created by Light Matters/Pixel Envy and composited into the live-action footage.

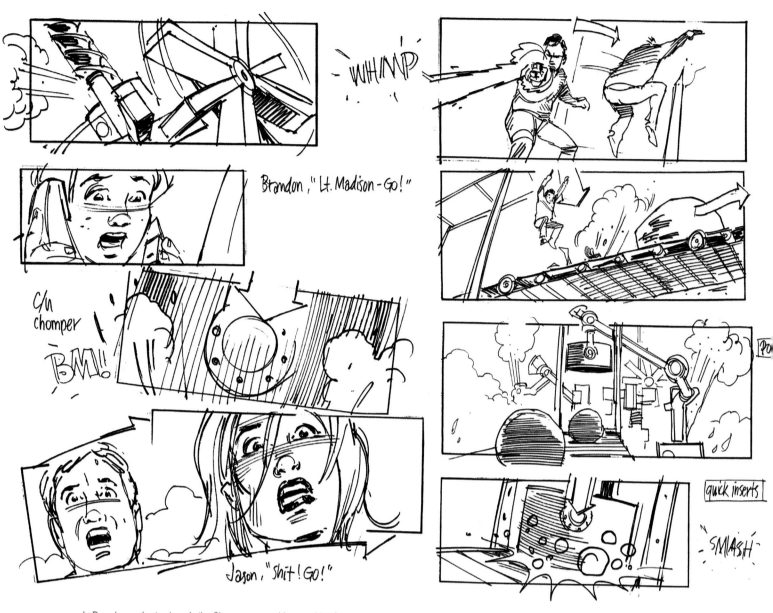

In Dave Lowery's storyboards the Chompers resemble something from a steam-powered factory.

Jason to simply calculate the timing in his head. "How could I dramatize that instant of decision? Jason needs an expert – so he calls the true expert Brandon, who, with his gang, has to figure out the pattern of the Chompers."

Gordon's original concept was even more over-the-top than the action ultimately seen on screen. "I wrote a whole series of absurdly mounting hazards that Gwen and Jason would have to navigate to get through the device. It had blades, hydraulic crushers, acid, fire jets... pretty much everything I could think of. It didn't really relate to what the Chompers turned into, although I'm glad the flame-jets stayed in. But I'm a huge fan of the simplified final design. And I don't know what the scene would

have cost had they filmed it the way I wrote it!"

While the initial plan was to use practical Chompers for the sequence, it was deemed too risky to pull off successfully (though the final Chomper glimpsed behind the flames was a practical effect). Instead, Allen and Weaver were filmed in a corridor set and composited into computer-generated footage of pistons, pylons, and crushers. The latter were animated by FX studio Light Matters/Pixel Envy. "We wanted them to look shiny and metallic, but at the same time they needed to have different textures," says the studio's VFX supervisor Mat Beck. "If you look closely, the cylinders going up and down are like something you might see in a car shop; they're smooth and shiny. But the Chompers themselves are a little grittier.

By changing the textures, tweaking the motion blur, and adding in shadows and reflections of light sources we took on the set, we were able to get them to look real."

The Chompers were animated by *Skyline* co-director Colin Strause and composited in to match Allen and Weaver's eyelines. Weaver's blonde wig posed certain challenges during the rotoscoping process. "We developed in-house techniques to gently blend hair back over the top of a background, because trying to simply put blonde hair in through a matte made it look clunky and cut out," says Beck.

FLAMES AND OOZE

Beck worked with special effects supervisor Matt Sweeney to shoot live-action footage of the flame-jets, which were composited into the final part of the sequence. "I kept saying, 'Just a little more flames, just a little more flames,' until someone came up to me and said, 'We need to shut this down or we're going to set the stage on fire!'"

One neat detail incorporated into the shot is the blaster crushed by a piston, which was realized with one of Jerry Moss's props. The blue ooze seen seeping out of the gun as it is smashed was intended to suggest the fantastical advanced science behind the surface of the Thermians' technology. ✦

The Chompers were enhanced with reflections of light sources taken on set.

THE ORIGINAL CHOMPERS

Audiences are briefly treated to shots of the glorious cardboard-looking Chompers in the original show, which were brought to life by production designer Linda DeScenna and her crew. "I imagined that the writer of the show was typing out that Chompers scene in exhausted desperation, late at night, on short deadline," says Robert Gordon. "A plot device that would be sufficient for a *Galaxy Quest* episode, where it was expected to have one repeat and never be seen again. But, of course, the writer could never have imagined his creations would be turned into real-life perils."

For Gordon there was a particular joy in seeing his old-school Chompers realized on screen. "I wrote something like, 'Jason is chased through the Chompers by a fish-headed alien monster before the alien is knocked into a vat of fake-looking lava.' And that's actually what they did! It was just so delightful and bizarre."

MANSER

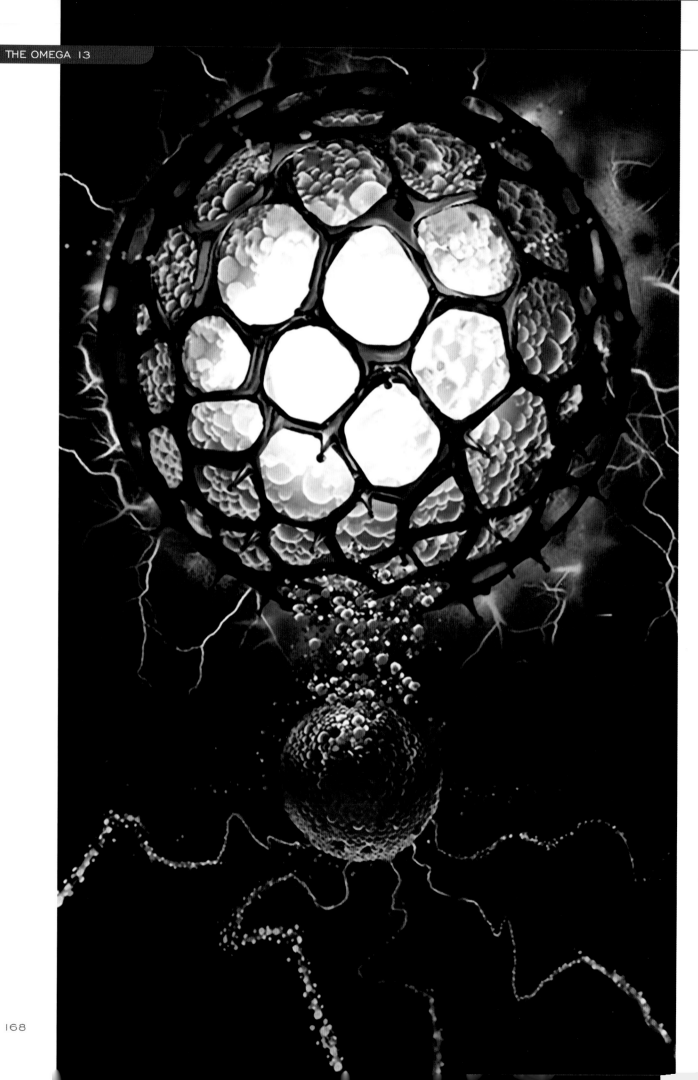

THE OMEGA 13

Figuring out how to visualize the mysterious time-warping device
proved a significant design challenge, as ILM's VFX team explain.

THE MATTER-REARRANGING OMEGA 13 was inspired by two of Robert Gordon's favorite Charlton Heston movies. Its name was a homage to the 1971 classic, *The Omega Man*, while Jason's tortuous crawl to activate the device was influenced by Heston's dying astronaut triggering the nuke at the climax of *Beneath the Planet of the Apes*.

Of course, the Omega 13 is much more inscrutable than a nuke. And just as the crew of the *Protector* have no idea what the Omega 13 actually does for the majority of the movie, for a long time no one involved in making *Galaxy Quest* was sure what the Omega 13 should look like. Gordon's initial script specified that its "center is a spinning cyclotron of energy" – but how that translated to screen was something that no one could agree upon. "It was a big thing that never really got sorted out until we were well until production," recalls Kim Bromley, ILM's visual effects producer. "The script was fairly vague, and there was a big change of ideas about what it was near the end."

According to ILM's visual effects art director, Alex Jaeger, the conceptual change came from a note from executive producer Steven Spielberg that made them rethink their design. "Steven wanted something even more outlandish and crazy than we had," he says.

"I believe the quote from Spielberg was, 'It should look like a Georgia O'Keeffe painting mixed with a Frank Gehry piece of architecture.' We were like, 'OK, sure – um, what's that?'"

Visual effects supervisor Bill George agrees that the Omega 13 posed one of the biggest conceptual challenges on the movie. "I think ultimately we thought, let's create some cool shit and hope for the best."

MOLECULAR BIOLOGY

With a couple of months left on the picture, only a skeleton crew at ILM were still working on the picture, meaning the company needed to employ freelance artists to work up new concepts. "The Omega 13 really jacked up the cost as I couldn't amortize it over the course of the show," says Bromley. "In the end the studio came up with the money, but it was expensive. I remember DreamWorks being very unhappy with me!"

One of the freelancers ILM brought in was concept artist James Clyne. After trying to process the enormity of the brief he was given ("They wanted something that had never been seen before, which is essentially impossible"), he began leafing through science books

Opposite page: James Clyne's conceptual design. Above: The Omega 13 is activated in a sequence that pays homage to *Beneath the Planet of the Apes*.

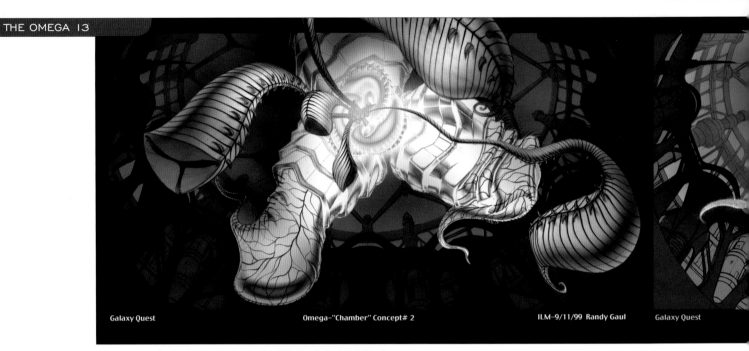

Galaxy Quest   Omega-"Chamber" Concept# 2   ILM–9/11/99 Randy Gaul   Galaxy Quest

Three concepts for the Omega 13 chamber by ILM's Randy Gaul and Alex Jaeger.

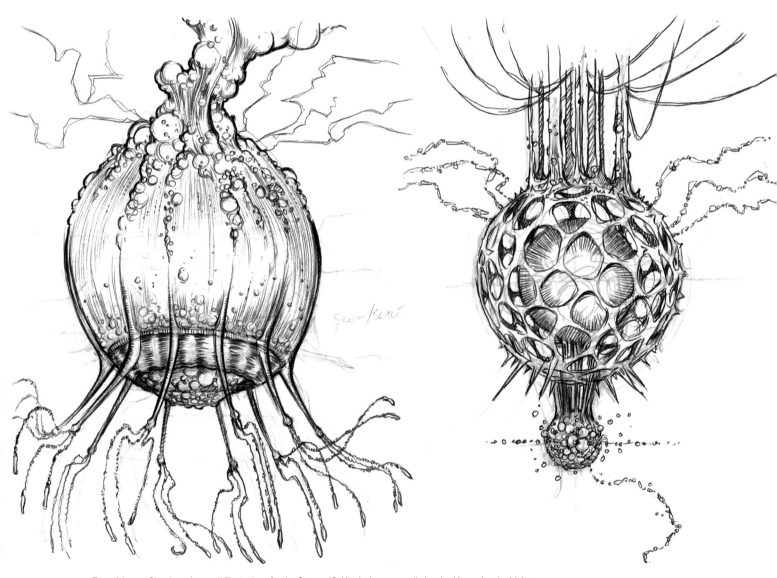

Two of James Clyne's early pencil illustrations for the Omega 13. His design was partly inspired by molecular biology.

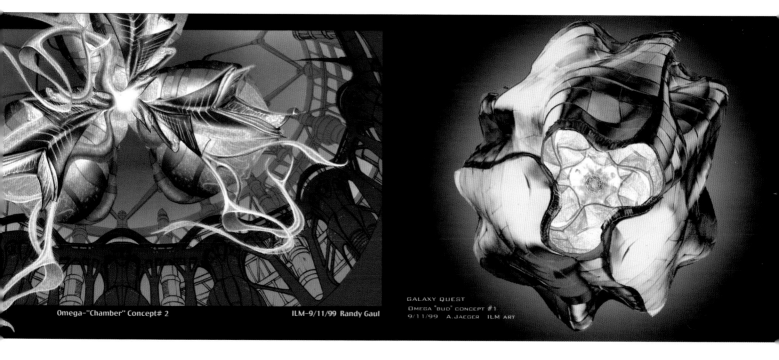

Omega-"Chamber" Concept# 2   ILM-9/11/99 Randy Gaul

GALAXY QUEST
OMEGA "BUD" CONCEPT #1
9/11/99 A.JAEGER ILM ART

for interesting shapes that might suit the device. "I was looking for something that would indicate its ability to transform energy. Based on a few discussions with ILM, I started looking at things like molecular biology and photomicrography. I was looking at what a cell looks like and what an atom looks like. A lot of those things are interesting shapes. I mean, they're part of our everyday biological makeup and familiar to us in a way, but at the same time they have this strange kind of look to them. ILM seemed to like the idea and I began working up a series of pencil sketches. My final design composited photomicrography into the image."

BRAIN AND TENDRILS

The Omega 13 did not entirely have to be reworked from scratch. The design, which would ultimately be computer generated, needed to connect to a lens-shaped prop that would be used during filming. "I did these snakelike tendrils that would kind of come off that practical prop piece," says Clyne. "Then it would connect to this big spherical brainlike thing. But we were really under the gun in terms of having to come up with the design, create it in CG, and then animate it. It had to be something that was simple and quick – it couldn't be some furry creature!"

When it came to translating Clyne's concept into CGI, technical director Aron Bonar created a program that made simulated particle shapes follow in the path of animated tendrils. Clyne's "spherical brainlike thing," meanwhile, was digitally painted by artist Ron Woodall. Interestingly, the look of the Omega 13 was also influenced by ILM's work on an abandoned sequence in which a wall panel comes off during the climactic battle with Sarris, according to ILM's associate visual effects supervisor, Ben Snow. "The idea was you'd

see this crazy, almost Giger-esque mechanical/organic stuff going on behind there... The filmmakers decided not to proceed with that gag. However, when we had to come up with something for the Omega 13 in a few weeks, it became an inspiration for the look."

"The science behind *Star Trek* is something that's always interested me, and with *Galaxy Quest* it was all about pulling off the science," adds Clyne. "In this case, it really worked out. It was great seeing the actual design in the film." ✦

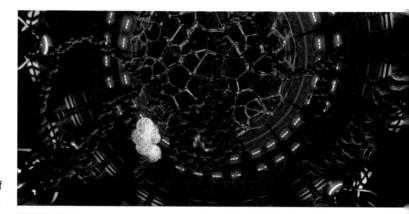

The "chamber" scene included animated spheres and tendrils, and a painted cage.

Composer and orchestrator David Newman. As well as composing the score, Newman has conducted live orchestras at screenings of the movie across the world.

ADVENTURES IN MUSIC

Galaxy Quest's composer David Newman explains why he wrote two versions of the title theme and recalls how he faced a race against time to compose the final cue for the movie.

COMPOSING THE MAJORITY OF THE score to *Galaxy Quest* was "easy," David Newman insists. After the composer was brought onto the film late in postproduction, he was happy to find that Dean Parisot and the producers loved the cues he wrote for the movie, and very little needed to be changed. "I got the movie and understood its tone," he says. "We hit upon the music right away at the beginning, which sometimes happens." The smoothness of the process made it even more of a shock when composing the cue for the final act suddenly became one of the biggest challenges of Newman's career.

The tone for Newman's score was established during the first piece of music he wrote for the film: the main title. In fact, he wrote two different versions of the theme for the filmmakers to choose from.

"The first piece I wrote was very much like the Alexander Courage title theme for the original series of *Star Trek*. It was kind of funny. But they liked the second one, and that's what went in the movie."

This second, less parodic theme still had a *Star Trek* link, having been partly inspired by Jerry Goldsmith's music for 1979's *Star Trek: The Motion Picture*, which Newman had worked on as a violinist early in his career. "I was there for all the sessions with Jerry Goldsmith," Newman says. "Jerry originally wrote all this music for the film but they [director Robert Wise and editor Todd Ramsay] threw it out, so he came back a month later [to rewrite it]. Jerry said he knew they wanted a swashbuckling score like *Star Wars*, he just didn't want to do that! Eventually he *did* do something like that, though, and we were just riffing off that main theme [in *Galaxy Quest*]. We basically

The cue "Revealing the Universe" plays when Jason is first encased by a Jell-O pod. Other cues include "Pathetic Nesmith," "Jason Takes Action," and "Angry Sarris."

Jason gazes out upon the universe from the starport. The cues that played during sequences such as this came together easily and were readily approved.

scored *Galaxy Quest* like the *Star Trek* movie but added a full choir.
We tried not to do too much goofy stuff." The main score would be
tweaked very slightly for the *Galaxy Quest* show-within-the-show,
which was played by a smaller orchestra.

By this point, Newman had worked on numerous comedies,
including *Bill and Ted's Excellent Adventure*, *The War of the Roses*,
and *The Nutty Professor*, and he knew one of the pitfalls of scoring
a movie in the genre. "The issue with scoring movies where people
are going to laugh at stuff is really tricky. You can't make somebody
laugh with music – but it's very easy to stifle a laugh with music. It's
not easy to [give space for] a laugh without suggesting, 'This is where
you laugh.' You need to stay on the fence – lean one way and then
another, but always stay on the fence. But then you need to move
[from comedy] into those more heartfelt moments. I learned how to
do that on *Throw Momma from the Train*. By the last act of *Galaxy
Quest,* the film becomes less about one-liners and more about the
group coming together, and the music helps allow that to develop."

RACE AGAINST TIME
Scoring that last act of *Galaxy Quest* – or, more precisely, the final
cue, which plays as the *Protector*'s bridge crash-lands while Brandon
and other fans light Roman candles – marked the point where, for one
evening at least, everything went wrong. "It was late at night and they
[Dean Parisot, Don Zimmerman, and the producers] were in their last
day of dubbing at Skywalker Sound. I had to be finished that evening
with the cue. So I played it for them – and they didn't like it."

Newman's credits range from *Anastasia* to Spielberg's *West Side Story*.

The muted reception to Newman's final cue couldn't have come at a worse time. The film was due to be print-mastered the next day so that all music, dialogue, and sound effects would be composited into a single soundtrack, and the process couldn't be delayed without costing a huge amount of money. Newman had the rest of the evening to fix the problem. "There wasn't the opportunity to go home, rewrite it, and come back. I was at the Fox scoring stage with 60 singers and an orchestra of 80 or 90 sat there waiting for me to tell them what to do."

Newman soon realized where he had made a mistake. "I figured out what was wrong and what they wanted me to do. The theme was too slow and militaristic. It didn't feel glorious or cathartic. I really had made an error, and it would have been bad to have the cue the way I originally did it. I sped it up and they liked it faster. But now I had to add 40 or 50 bars – which isn't easy!" Undeterred, Newman sat down at the piano and, section by section, began adding bars, working with the orchestra to perfect the timing.

Surprisingly perhaps, Newman doesn't look back on the experience with a shudder – far from it. "Sitting there at the piano playing it for the orchestra was exhilarating. It was one of the best experiences I've ever had, coming from a place of absolute terror. And the cue turned out great – probably one of the best pieces of writing I've ever done."

Newman's experience of *Galaxy Quest* didn't end once he had submitted his final score. He has conducted live orchestras at screenings of *Galaxy Quest* several times in the intervening years, and always takes pride in the rapturous reception that the movie and its score receives. "The film really holds up. It gets such a wonderful response with the audience laughing through the whole film, and the orchestra gets a wonderful response, too. It's so thrilling to do it. If you do enough movies, once in a while you have an experience like *Galaxy Quest*. There's something special about it." ✦

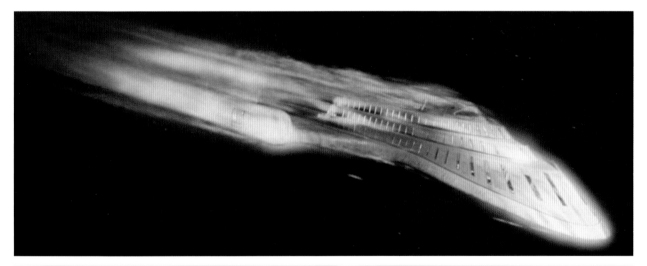

The fans guide the *Protector*'s bridge section to the convention center. Newman realized that his final cue needed to be faster, more glorious, and cathartic.

THE ART OF NOISE

Sound designer Richard Beggs reminisces about crafting
Galaxy Quest's scrapes, snuffles, clunks, and thunks.

"**I** DON'T OFTEN GET TO WORK ON outrageous pictures like this," says Richard Beggs. "If I had been offered *Star Wars*, I'm not sure I would have taken it; it's just not my temperament. But there was something about *Galaxy Quest* that appealed to my sense of humor. Plus it had a lot of heart. It was a very sweet movie in the best sense of the word."

Galaxy Quest was not *entirely* unfamiliar territory for Beggs. He had, after all, previously worked on the sci-fi comedies *Spaceballs* and *Critters*, as well as *Ghostbusters*, another film to artfully blend genres. But this is just a tiny part of a long career that has taken in everything from *Apocalypse Now* (for which he landed an Oscar®) to *Lost in Translation* and *Rain Man*. The latter was one of his frequent collaborations with producer Mark Johnson, who brought him on board *Galaxy Quest* once shooting was already underway.

The sound design for the spaceships was, it turns out, the easy part. "It was fairly conventional spaceship sounds that fit the mold of the TV shows the picture is sending up, such as the doors that sound like a smooth zipper when they open. I made them – or sweetened them with – custom effects to give them the gloss they needed. But there were several things I thought were funny. When the ship leaves the spaceport and there's that long, sustained scraping sound... I took a big ride cymbal and dampened it so it wouldn't ring. Then I scratched it and expanded [the sound] with different tools until I found something that gave me the right effect. I liked that contrast of the unpleasant, scratchy metal with all that technology."

Beggs's other favorite *Protector* sound is more subtle: the noise of the ship's engines cutting out after the beryllium sphere is damaged by a Tothian mine. "It's one of my favorite sounds and

The audio design of the *Protector* was based on classic TV spaceship sounds, which were enhanced with subtly manipulated effects.

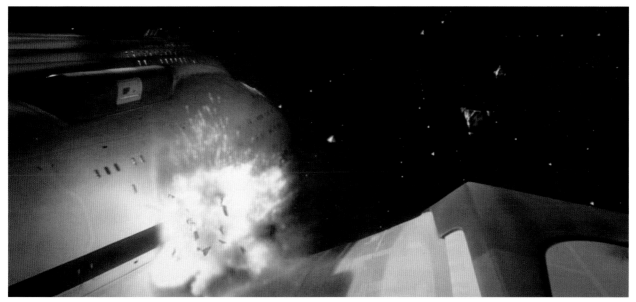

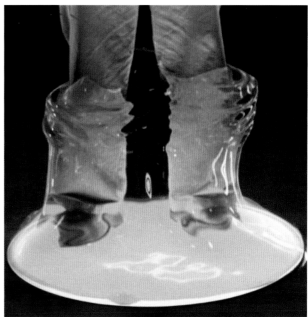

The exploding mines, pig lizard's snuffles, and squelching of the Jell-O pods were just three of the sounds that Beggs created for the movie.

one most people don't even notice. I manipulated one of my library sounds to create that simple, limp, sputtery noise. It's like the sound a ladyfinger firecracker makes as it fails – the fuse fizzes, then the powder goes *put-put-put*. For a few seconds [in the sequence] there's no music and you just hear that dejected sound. It has no glamor, no action, no excitement, but emotionally it fits the scene."

MONSTER SOUNDS

The sound of *Galaxy Quest*'s spaceships interested Beggs less than some of the film's other more unusual noises, not least the voices of the movie's magnificent monsters. Beggs remembers

spending hours listening to all manner of snuffling, snorting, and grunting to get the sound of the pig lizard just right. "I combined several different pigs to make that guy!"

Then there was the rock monster, which posed one of the movie's biggest challenges. "Rattle, scrape, and clunk – those are the three basic elements of that thing, that's its voice. But it took a long time to get that thing to sound even halfway decent. I didn't have the sound of boulders and I wasn't going to go out to Bryce Canyon National Park, move a 20-ton boulder and record it. And it was hard to do because there's this issue of physical mass and sheer weight. I had some spare 10-pound cobblestones in my backyard so I thought, 'Ooh, this will be the perfect sound.' So I began hitting them against each other, rolling them around, and recording them with a very high-end recorder and microphone. But it sounded really wimpy! It was just *click-click-click*. But then when I dropped them on this concrete area in my backyard, it sounded much better. Especially on thinner parts of the concrete, because the earth underneath the concrete imparted this low-frequency component that gave it a sense of mass. Then a friend and colleague of mine, [sound designer and director] Gary Rydstrom, sent me some raw rock sounds he had from a movie he'd done with a landslide or something. So it was a combination of my sounds and his."

JELLY AND ANVILS

Another aspect of the movie that required a homemade solution was the Jell-O pods that the crew use to travel to the Thermian space station. "I had this weird powder that you mixed with water to get this thick, viscous stuff. It was like Jell-O, and I mixed it in a big tub. It sounded horrible [during sound experiments] and it was all done by hand."

If the pods needed to be soft and gooey, then the sound of the Chompers needed to be hard and unforgiving. "I didn't want it to sound sci-fi or at all electronic," says Beggs, "I wanted it to sound more like an industrial version of a blacksmith shop. I just thought it was more interesting for it to have this Earthbound quality – it made it sound more dangerous, you know what I mean? I had recordings of a very heavy hammer hitting an anvil. But the size of these things

is important. A small anvil goes *tink* – and the Chompers can't go *tink*! The damn thing has to weigh at least 40 or 50 pounds or more. You have to deal with physics. It needed a 10-pound sledge [hammer] hitting a very heavy anvil to get the sound I wanted."

The appearance and physical nature of the pods and the Chompers at least offered a starting point for what they might sound like. Inventing the sound of the Omega 13, on the other hand, was far from obvious. "To me it was the sound that was most important in the movie – and perhaps the biggest problem," Beggs recalls. "It looks like a nest of little balls that are sort of suspended magnetically in front of you and they whirl around. What sound would that make? I probably messed with that for two or three days – for something that lasts a few seconds! I was determined I wasn't going to borrow any sounds. It had to be as original as I could make, yet still somehow sound like what it was. I wanted them to have this rhythmic sound, almost like billiard balls moving really fast."

So how did Beggs come up with the original, otherworldly sound of the Omega 13? His answer is as mysterious as the device itself. "I'm sorry to disappoint you but I can't remember!" he laughs. "But they should have played it louder in the film."

For all of Beggs' inventive audio solutions, one of his favorite sounds in the picture was actually made by an actor rather than himself. "That horrible sound that the Thermians make is absolutely terrific," he says, launching into a pretty convincing impersonation of Laliari's screech. "It makes your hair stand up straight, right? I couldn't top that. It's out of this world." ✦

The sound of Gorignak was devised through a mix of rocks dropped on concrete and effects provided by seven-time Oscar® winner Gary Rydstrom.

Top: The examination scene featured an array of manipulated sound effects. Above: Creating the sound design for the mysterious Omega 13 was one of the film's biggest challenges.

THE CUTTING ROOM

Galaxy Quest was cut into a tight, thrilling "ride movie" during postproduction,
but a last-minute drive to give it family appeal led to some frantic re-editing.

"**Y**OU LOOK AT DON ZIMMERMAN'S resume, and you can't replicate something like that," says line producer Charles Newirth. He's not wrong. In Zimmerman's 50-year (then 30-year) career, he has cut multiple movies for Hal Ashby, Sylvester Stallone, and Tom Shadyac among others, giving him vast experience of editing both character-driven comedies and action-driven spectaculars.

Zimmerman immediately hit it off with Dean Parisot, leading to a working relationship that has continued through all of Parisot's subsequent movies. "Dean calls me 'The Hammer' because I have such a strong feeling about things and can tolerate less than he does," Zimmerman laughs. All of which suggests that the postproduction of *Galaxy Quest* was a straightforward affair – which was far from the case.

The editing process began traditionally enough, with Parisot and Zimmerman pulling together a rough assembly with temp music and incomplete VFX. "I try to cut relatively tight, and Dean doesn't shoot excessive amounts," says Zimmerman. "The first cut, or editor's assembly, includes every scene before you start whittling it down to make it really slick. It's like sculpting."

Zimmerman estimates that this first rough assembly clocked in at around two hours, though others remember it as somewhat longer. "It was probably two hours and 45 minutes," says ILM's Rebel Mac supervisor, Stu Maschwitz. "It seemed to me that was predominantly because of Sam Rockwell's hilarious ad-libs. He was the star of that version of the film! I'm sure they had to make

The movie's bad language was trimmed as the edit changed from PG-13 to PG.

The scene in which Quellek introduces Alexander to his "bathroom" was cut from the movie.

the gut-wrenching decision to remove all these hilarious things that he had said or done."

Regardless of how long the rough cut was, Zimmerman (assisted by sons Dean and Dan) and Parisot began the work of paring it down. Certain sequences were trimmed for timing, while others were cut altogether, including the sight of Alexander Dane's alarming toilet and Dian Bachar's nervous techie offering up his explanation for strange proton surges (both scenes are thankfully available as DVD extras).

As usual, they received notes from the studio executives. Visual effects producer Robert Stadd remembers watching a two-and-a-half-hour test screening that was attended by DreamWorks executive Jeffrey Katzenberg. "Jeffrey said, 'It's got to be a ride film.' Dean and Don kept working at it, making it sharper and sharper, and it really came together in the last few weeks of post. What you see on the screen is so tight now."

Parisot wasn't entirely convinced about all of the studio notes he received, however – especially one shot of Jason's limo lifting off while he's asleep. Originally the film was supposed to cut from Jason nodding off to him awakening on the Thermian starport, imbuing the sequence with more of a dreamlike quality, but DreamWorks wanted to make it clearer from the get-go. "That was one of the only things that they asked for and we added," recalls Zimmerman.

The limo lift-off sequence – shot in a tiny alley near Paramount Studios – was a late addition.

TESTING TIME

Eventually, Parisot and Zimmerman had a cut of the film that they, and the film's producers, were happy with. A test screening was arranged in Burbank. Sound designer Richard Beggs remembers being in the car with Parisot as they passed the recruited audience standing in line. "Dean got this look upon his face," he says. "There were all these parents with little children in the line. This was *not* the target audience at that point. He realized immediately that this was the audience that the studio wanted the movie to be acceptable to..."

It emerged that DreamWorks hoped to pivot *Galaxy Quest* into a family movie that could compete with Sony's *Stuart Little* (released one week before *Galaxy Quest*) and draw in the crowds who had flocked to *The Santa Clause*. The problem was that Parisot had never set out to make a family film. The first cut had violence, it

had swearing, it had innuendo. *Stuart Little* it was not.

The first non-PG test screening received a mixed reaction from the family audience in attendance. Beggs remembers that viewers largely responded favorably – but things became rather more heated once the lights went up. "We were stood talking and a woman suddenly came up to Dean," Beggs recalls. "She laid into him saying, 'How dare you expose my child to this kind of movie. It's completely inappropriate!' He was pinned to the wall and was like, 'Help! Get me out of here!' It was just insane, you know?"

"I was trying to make a story with characters who had grounded lives and I think they [the studio] saw it as a Christmas movie with Tim Allen," explains Parisot. "They had been making *Gladiator*, which was a huge undertaking and had gone way over budget. So everybody was concentrating on that and left us lunatics alone for a long time.

Don Zimmerman seamlessly blended the movie's serious and comic moments in a way that never felt jarring. The Mak'tar fan above was played by Bill Chott.

The final cut of the movie was much tighter than the first assembly and felt like a "ride" movie.

Then when they saw the first version, they were like, 'Wait, we can't do this. We're making a Christmas movie for kids!'"

It was clear to everyone that further judicious editing was required to secure the necessary PG rating. Despite the filmmakers' surprise at having to tone down the movie, editing out the adult material was not actually an insurmountable challenge. Most of the violence and innuendo trimmed from the film didn't impact on the story, although losing the sequence in which Gwen entices two of Sarris's guards forward to their doom left some viewers puzzled as to why the character's top suddenly becomes unzipped.

The most infamous edit, however, was when Gwen's "Well, fuck that!" response to the Chompers was replaced by the far gentler "Well, screw that." The fact that Parisot had not shot an alternative PG-friendly take and had to rely on not-entirely-convincing ADR is testament to how it never crossed the minds of those working on the picture that they were making something with family appeal. "I still think that Sigourney coming round the corner and saying, 'Well, fuck

that!' would have been one of the biggest laughs of all time," says line producer Charles Newirth. "But I'm glad that we dubbed it badly, which was intentional on Dean's part!"

While there still remains some disappointment over the sequences that were cut or redubbed, everyone agrees that the PG edit didn't detract from the film's considerable achievements. If anything, it was surprisingly effective as a family-friendly movie. "It really needed to be aged up not down, but ironically it plays very well for a young audience," admits producer Mark Johnson.

The movie's writer also remains pleasantly surprised at how it became an unexpected family favorite. "I don't miss it [the more adult material]," says Robert Gordon. "I like that kids can watch it with their families and I love hearing kids say, 'Never give up, never surrender' and 'By Grabthar's hammer' and all of those things."

But if the new edits were made to widen *Galaxy Quest*'s appeal, the promotion of the movie did little to help the film find the mass audience everyone felt it deserved... ✦

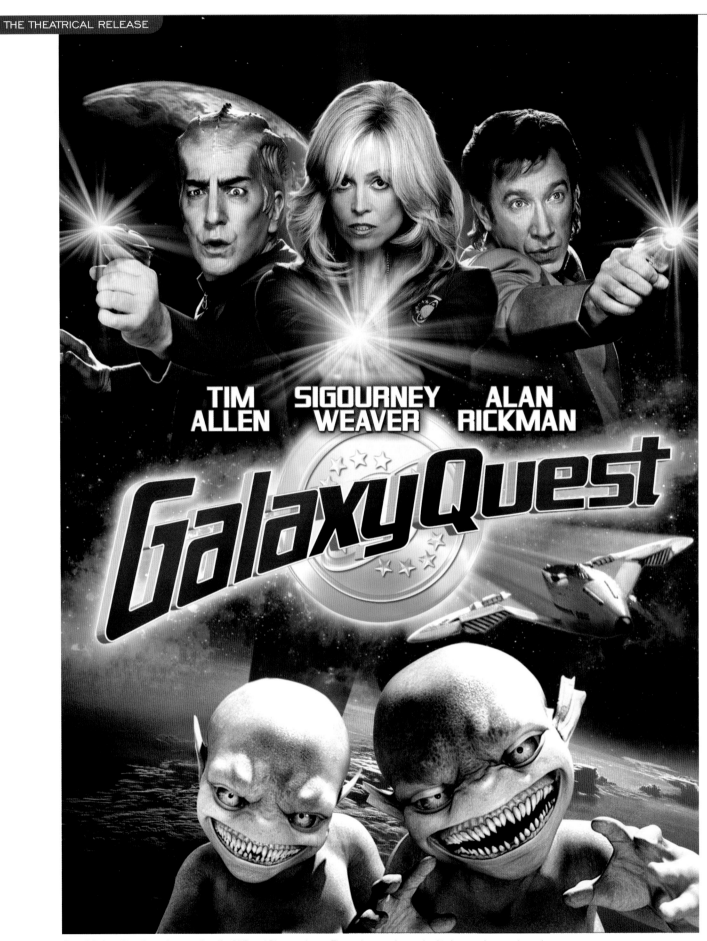

One of *Galaxy Quest*'s posters, used on the DVD and Blu-ray release. The early campaign evolved to become less wacky and more grown-up.

THE THEATRICAL RELEASE

Galaxy Quest found an appreciative audience on its initial release. But might it have become a genuine box office sensation if it had been promoted differently?

Galaxy Quest WAS RELEASED IN cinemas on Christmas Day 1999, having been pushed back from its original release date of December 10, 1999 during postproduction. It would be wrong to say that the movie flopped when it opened; this was no replay of *The Thing* or *Fight Club* – indifferently received box office bombs that only later became highly regarded. Reviews of *Galaxy Quest* were broadly positive, with *Variety* describing

it as "a mischievously clever and slickly commercial sci-fi comedy with strong cross-generational appeal," and *The Washington Post* praising its ability to "poke wicked fun at *Star Trek* and its devotees, while at the same time serving up sincere homage to the beloved sci-fi serial."

It was a moderate commercial hit too, bringing in $7,012,630 during its opening weekend and remaining in the top 10 for the next nine weeks. Yet the filmmakers wondered if it would have

ILM's visual effects crew sign, encapsulating some of the movie's most iconic images.

attracted a much wider audience if there had been a different approach to the marketing. "We couldn't locate the sweet spot to get the movie out to an audience," says executive producer Elizabeth Cantillon. "It was Christmas, it was very competitive, and there was a Robin Williams movie [*Bicentennial Man*] out at the same time. We didn't find it in the marketing."

"*Galaxy Quest* did well, but it should have done twice the business," adds producer Mark Johnson. "It seemed to me that it was sold a little like a 'Tim Allen comedy' – and a lot of Tim Allen comedies had done very well, of course. But this was different... I don't think DreamWorks realized quite what they were getting. I don't think they realized how funny it was and how well it worked with an audience until late in the game. But by that time, the decisions about when to release it and the advertising campaign had been made."

The fact that the film found any kind of appreciative audience was down to viewers recommending it to friends and family, argues Dean Parisot. "*Galaxy Quest* made almost exactly the same four or five weekends in a row, which as I understand it, proved it was making money based on word-of-mouth rather than the advertising," he says. "They [marketed it] for kids, but adults were showing up in droves. They didn't expect that... I actually got a call from Jeffrey Katzenberg, who apologised, saying, 'I'm sorry, you and Mark Johnson were right. We didn't get the advertising right.' But it's hard to be angry about it now. They just didn't [realize the depth] of the fanboy and fangirl culture."

THE CAMPAIGN

Unusually, less than one month after the film's release, Johnson and DreamWorks' then head of marketing, Terry Press (who, as Johnson makes clear, is a good friend) debated at UCLA how the film was promoted, excerpts of which were published in the *LA Times*. During the debate, Press admitted that the complex story, along with the fact they couldn't legally suggest it was a *Star Trek* parody, made the campaign tricky. "We did believe in the movie or we wouldn't have released it at Christmas," she pointed out. "It is a very clever movie but the message was, in some ways, difficult to tell...We literally looked at 300 different posters trying to convey the right tone for all audiences we believed would want to see this great little movie. Do I think we nailed it? No. But like everything else with this movie, we simply ran out of time."

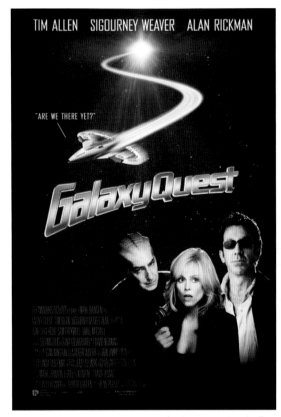 

An original *Galaxy Quest* poster; image of a "lost episode" on the *Travis Latke* site using comic art designed by Warren Manser for the convention sequences.

Another of *Galaxy Quest*'s original poster designs; a billboard in Hollywood – which went up while the movie was still being finished.

It's easy to overlook the fact that, even if the campaign had its flaws, the studio *did* employ some inventive promotional concepts. First, there was the *Travis Latke's Galaxy Quest Page* website. Boasting deliberately outmoded graphics and a mind-scrambling jumble of fonts, the site was "written" by fictional uber-fan Latke and consisted of interviews with the stars of the TV show ("Perhaps we can go out for yoghurt tonight?" Travis suggests to an uneasy Jason) and crazed episode summaries. The website attracted a cult fanbase all of its own.

The film was also accompanied by the 25-minute tie-in mockumentary, *Galaxy Quest 20th Anniversary: The Journey Continues*, made for E! Television Network. The script was written by Andy Marx (grandson of Groucho), who wittily expanded on the history of the TV show. Marx remembers drawing on his own childhood memories to depict *Galaxy Quest*'s "legendary creator," Frank Ross. "My father [Arthur Marx] was a film and TV writer, and when I was growing up in the '60s, a lot of his friends were also writers, many of whom lived in our neighborhood," he says. "So there were plenty of them around the house when I was growing up. Frank Ross was kind of an amalgamation of many of them. And one of my father's writer friends was a great guy named Frank Moss [writer on *Wagon Train*, *The Lone Ranger,* and many other shows], who was very encouraging to me when I was starting to write. I think I based the name on him, changing 'Moss' to 'Ross.'" As well as featuring the movie's cast reprising their roles, the mockumentary had cameos from the production crew, including Mark Johnson and Charles Newirth as TV historians.

Marx's mockumentary hinted that, like *Star Trek*, *Galaxy Quest* was a show with the potential to be extended into a fully fledged franchise that could expand upon its mythology. Both cast and crew were in agreement that the material seemed ripe for a sequel or spin-off TV show. But developing a follow-up proved to be no easy task. ✦

GALAXY QUEST
THE LEGACY

In the two decades following *Galaxy Quest*'s release, its status as a cult classic has been cemented, with the movie inspiring fansites, models, comics, and cosplay groups.

IF *GALAXY QUEST* ENJOYED MODEST success in cinemas, it finally fulfilled its smash-hit potential when it was unleashed on home video in May 2000. On viewing it on VHS or DVD, many who had missed – or perhaps even dismissed – it during its theatrical run found a deeper, richer movie than they might have expected. "It did much better during its home theater run than in the theater," says executive producer Elizabeth Cantillon. "I'm glad that it found an audience. It was so weird and fresh and fun."

While the movie may have been overlooked at the Oscars®, it earned its fair share of official recognition over the course of 2000. Tim Allen landed a Saturn Award for Best Actor, and the film secured a host of other Saturn nominations, from Best Makeup and Best Special Effects to Best Director and Best Costume. Meanwhile, Dean Parisot, Robert Gordon, and David Howard won Best Dramatic Presentation at that year's Hugo Awards.

In the years that followed, comic-cons and cosplay became much more mainstream, and the film's celebration of fan culture resonated

Galaxy Quest fans, the Thermians from Utah, at FanX comic-con in Salt Lake City, 2019; IDW's 2008 comic series *Galaxy Quest: Global Warning!*.

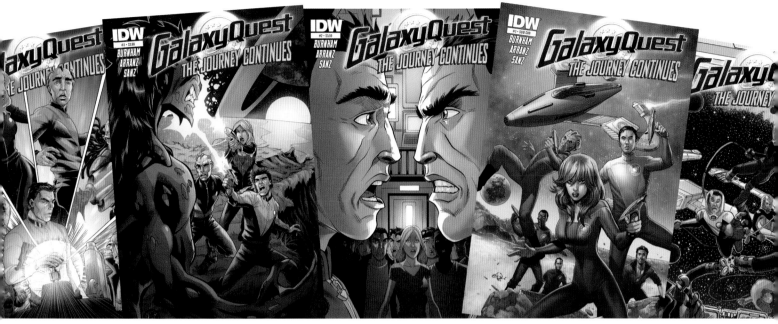

IDW's 2015 comic series *Galaxy Quest: The Journey Continues*. The comic was written by Erik Burnham with art by Nacho Arranz.

more than ever. "I don't think there had ever been this kind of movie, where the fans were celebrated," says Robert Gordon. "Fandom has changed so much now. I always hoped the movie would age well, but I never thought it would be the norm that fans would become the cool guys, you know? That certainly wasn't the case with me growing up, when I was one of those geeks reading books about the making of *Star Trek* and *2001* or watching any science fiction movie that came out. I think *Galaxy Quest* was on the edge of that moment [before fan culture became bigger], where fans could still be the underdogs."

The film's "Questarian" fanbase can be seen in the amount of official and unofficial tie-ins, events, and merchandise that has accrued. There have been fansites (*The Questarian*, *Galaxy Request*, *Galaxy Quest Fan*, and many others), fan-produced dramas (courtesy of Fictionshed), licensed models from Pegasus Toys, and prints by Mondo, while IDW expanded the universe with two comic-book series (2008's *Galaxy Quest: Global Warning!* and 2015's *Galaxy Quest: The Journey Continues*). David Newman has even conducted live orchestras to accompany screenings of the film. Meanwhile, famous fans have professed their love of the movie, from the stars of the *Star Trek* franchise to J.J. Abrams (who has described *Galaxy Quest* as one of his "favorite *Trek* films.")

So why did two decades pass without a sequel or spin-off? It almost happened during that time, more than once. In 2015, Robert Gordon, Dean Parisot, and Mark Johnson were in the process of developing a TV series for Amazon Studios. The cast were eager to climb aboard the *Protector* again. But then the unthinkable happened:

the death of Alan Rickman in 2016. In the immediate aftermath, the cast and crew couldn't imagine doing the show without their friend, especially as Alexander was such an integral character in the proposed spin-off. That wasn't the end of talk of a sequel, though, with comedian Paul Scheer writing a new version in 2017 and Mark Johnson developing another concept with Simon Pegg in 2021.

NEVER SURRENDER

One thing is clear: the love of *Galaxy Quest* isn't going away any time soon. In 2019, Screen Junkies released the well-received *Never Surrender: A Galaxy Quest Documentary*, which delved into the making of the movie, as well as profiling its Thermian-cosplaying fans. "When I first saw *Galaxy Quest*, the day after Christmas, I thought it was going to be a kinda funny movie," says the documentary's director, Jack Bennett. "But it's one of those movies where after you see it, you're like, 'Wait, that was *really* good, right?' Then when it came out on DVD, I must have seen it 100 times." It took three years from Bennett's initial pitch to his producers to the documentary's release. "Every time I thought I couldn't take fighting to get the movie out into the world, I would hear the line, 'Never give up! Never surrender!' If Bob [Gordon] hadn't written that line, I might have given up two years earlier!"

During the making of the documentary, the devotion of *Galaxy Quest*'s fanbase became even more apparent when one of the producers spotted a couple ("The Thermians from Utah") dressed as Thermians at the SiliCon convention in San Jose. When Bennett

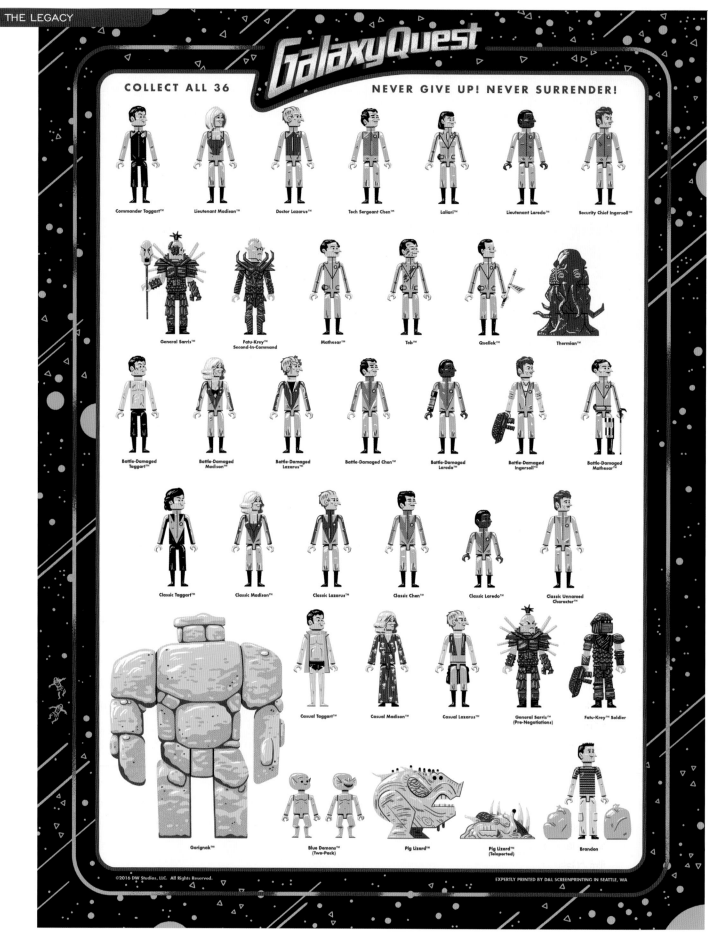

©2016 DW Studios, LLC. All Rights Reserved.

Galaxy Quest poster artwork by Andrew Kolb for the collectibles company, Mondo.

Galaxy Quest cosplayers Harold and Roxanne Weir; the poster for the 2019 film *Never Surrender: A Galaxy Quest Documentary*.

spoke to them, they refused to break character. "After that, we decided to open the documentary with these underdog fans, and end with the screening of *Galaxy Quest* that brought them together with the makers of the movie. They became the heart of the documentary."

Those two Thermians from Utah, Harold and Roxanne Weir, have spent over seven years involved in *Galaxy Quest* cosplay. While they both loved *Galaxy Quest* on its release, it wasn't until the 2014 FanX convention in Salt Lake City that they donned Thermian outfits for the first time. Harold admits that their first silver Thermian body suits were "awful," but adds that they immediately felt closer to the characters. "The funny thing is, I've always felt there is magic around *Galaxy Quest*," Harold says. "And when we dressed as Thermians, the magic got even more real…"

As their skills improved, the couple made realistic costumes for the command crew (including a mold of Dr. Lazarus's headpiece) and the Sarris Dominion. Every convention they attended would attract fans requesting photos or wanting to share their love of the film. "*Galaxy Quest* has endured for so long because it does what so many of us would love to see happen – 'It's all real!'" says Harold. "And it also shows there is a hero in all of us," Roxanne adds.

LIGHTNING IN A BOTTLE

Two decades on and counting, *Galaxy Quest* is widely viewed as both a comedy classic and, importantly, a science fiction classic. It's a fitting testament to the director and actors and writers and producers and costume department and artists and designers and stunt performers and hundreds of other talented individuals who channelled their energy and imagination into the movie.

"The fact that people still love it… it's so surreal to me," says Robert Gordon. "I'm still processing it. It's very fulfilling when people come up to me after hearing that I had something to do with it… Just the way they light up [talking] about it."

"I have a warm place in my heart for that movie," adds Dean Parisot. "I've stayed friends with almost everyone on it, and I felt like I made the movie I wanted to make – which is a hard thing to pull off. For me, the movie resonates because it's a love letter to fans, but it's also a love letter to the process [of moviemaking]: that ability to create these adventures that we wouldn't usually experience, and which we get to live out for an hour and a half. But I think it's lightning in a bottle when a movie keeps going like *Galaxy Quest* has. It's taken on a life of its own now." ✦

Copyright © 1999 Stan Winston Studio

Writer: Matt McAllister
Art Editor: Dan Rachael
Project Manager: Jo Bourne
Head of Development: Ben Robinson
Cover Illustration: Brian Williamson

Thanks to Brandon Alinger, Tim Allen, Andy Armstrong, John Barber, Mat Beck,
Richard Beggs, Jack Bennett, Don Bies, Simon Bisley, Patrick Breen, Brom,
Kim Bromley, Ronn Brown, Barney Burman, Lou Bustamante, Elizabeth Cantillon,
Jim Charmatz, Murray Close, James Clyne, Enrico Colantoni, Christian Colquhoun,
Fon Davis, Gina DeDomenico, Linda DeScenna, Max Dionne, David Dranitzke,
Guy Hendrix Dyas, Judy Elkins, Stefen Fangmeier, Randy Gaul, Bill George,
Dan B Goldman, John Goodson, Robert Gordon, Kirk Henderson, David Howard,
Jeremy Howard, Alex Jaeger, Benton Jew, Brad Johnson, Mark Johnson, Risa Kessler,
Richard Landon, Sabi Lofgren, Justin Long, David Lowery, Michael Lynch,
Shane Mahan, Warren Manser, Andy Marx, Stu Maschwitz, Robert Q. Mathews,
Mark 'Crash' McCreery, Daryl Mitchell, Rodney Montague, Simon Murton, Ve Neill,
Charles Newirth, David Newman, Michael Okuda, Dean Parisot, Neil Pearson,
Alice Peebles, Alan Peterson, Missi Pyle, Dylan Rachael, Jed Rees, The Alan Rickman
Estate, Erich Rigling, Sam Rockwell, John J. Rutchland III, Jordu Schell, Tony Shalhoub,
Ben Snow, Robert Stadd, Miles Teves, Pat Turner, Danny Wagner, Sigourney Weaver,
Harold and Roxanne Weir, Rainn Wilson, Sven Wilson, Tracey Wilson, Matt Winston,
Jerzy Zieliński, Don Zimmerman

Published by Hero Collector Books, a division of Eaglemoss Ltd. 2021
Premier Place, 2 & A Half Devonshire Square, EC2M 4UJ, London, UK.
All rights reserved.

Eaglemoss France, 144 Avenue Charles de Gaulle,
92200 Neuilly-Sur-Seine

TM Paramount Pictures. © 2021 DW Studios, LLC. All rights reserved.

Unit photography: Murray Close

ILM photos © Industrial Light & Magic. Used with permission.

All Stan Winston Studio concept design & behind-the-scenes images
appearing in this book are copyright © 1999 Stan Winston Studio.
All rights reserved.

www.herocollector.com

Illustration by Kirk Henderson / ILM ©